The Turning Point
Islam and Jesus' Salvation

FAWZY T. ABDELMALEK

Library of Congress Control Number: 2022942367
                    Paperback: 978-1-958169-26-1
                    eBook: 978-1-958169-27-8

CONTENTS

PART IV — THE WAY TO SALVATION

FOREWORD

A careful and prayerful study of the material contained in this book will prepare the reader to make intelligent and convincing choices on important issues that relate to religion and faith.

"*The Turning Point - Islam and Jesus' Salvation*" explores Islam's history, ideology, culture, struggles, and challenges. Is Islam in trouble? Is there an intellectual basis in the Quran to discredit the deity of Jesus Christ as the Son of God? Can a Muslim benefit from God's free offer of Salvation?

This book reflects an accurate image and presents in plain English facts that are extracted from historical sources, Islamic texts, book of the *Quran* and the *Ahadith* (sayings and traditions of the Prophet *Muhammad*). It may appear that some of the material contained in this book is likely to be tagged as racist or extreme, but the data is in fact genuine and as accurate as to the context in which it is represented. The book is completely truthful with no cover-ups or apologies to compromise with the views of Radical Islam.

Islam is a total way of life that affects how Muslims think and behave, whether they are in the mosque, the home, or the market place. Every area of human existence comes under the authority of Islam's law and ideology. Consequently, there is no separation between religion and politics in Islam. Islamic religion is supposed to inform and influence the political arena, Islamic *law*, or *Shariah* must be fully implemented as the law of the land so that all come under the authority of *Allah* and fully submit themselves to Him and His messenger *Muhammad*.

Extreme and radical Muslims believe that it is necessary that the state and its representatives not to hold views or engage in activities that go against the teachings of the Quran and Muhammad's *Ahadith* and *traditions*, which constitute the Islamic law, or *Shariah*. Democracy remains unrealized ideal within the Islamic countries that are ruled by the Islamic law.

Muhammad, the Prophet of Islam revealed in the Quran the evidence of the deity of *Jesus Christ*, yet he denied that Jesus is the Son of God and Savior of men. The evidence in the Quran confirming the deity of Jesus Christ is overwhelmingly conclusive to any honest objective seeker of the truth. Christians believe that God (*the Father*) appeared in the flesh (*the Son*) through His Spirit (*the Holy Spirit*).

In the Christian faith, the Father, the Son and the Holy Spirit are three attributes of one God and not three Gods! Muhammad who was raised among Jews and Christians did not accept Jesus Christ as his Savior and Lord, not because he was unable to understand, but most likely he had his own agenda and was simply unwilling to believe.

Likewise, many people of all dominations and faiths, Judaism, Christianity, Islam, and even atheists are confused about the nature of Jesus Christ, because they had never been willing to consider the claim of Jesus Christ of his own. They refuse to come to intellectual grips with the basic historical facts concerning His birth, life, teachings, miracles, death and resurrection.

They fear that they would be convinced, and as a result would have to change their way of life. Many who had the will to learn, have found the evidence so convincing that they have accepted the fact that Jesus Christ truly is who He claimed to be; the Son of God, and accepted Him as their own Savior and Lord. Majority of people in most cultures do not need to be convinced of His deity, nor of their need of Him as Savior, rather they need to be told how to receive Him as their Savior and Lord.

Thus, it is the Christian himself who will drive the greatest benefit from reading this book "*The Turning Point- Islam and Jesus' Salvation*". This book provides to the reader facts about Islam's historical, ideological, social, and spiritual knowledge that help to understand the other, and simultaneously strengthen their own faith in Jesus Christ. This book provides evidence material that will enable one to share his faith more effectively with others.

Sometimes it just amazes me that it is all here at hand. Salvation was not achievable before the death of Jesus Christ on the cross. God revealed himself, took our image and became man, incarnated in the person of Jesus Christ to lift us to him as his beloved children. He lived among us and died on the cross for the forgiveness of our sins. We are fortunate to have passion in life, but if we can make it safely to eternity then we are really lucky. We are all lucky that God loves us so much that he himself descended in the person of our Lord and Savior Jesus Christ for our sake. This book is written with conviction to enlighten the reader about Islam, and to understand what kind and depth of love that God offered his only begotten Son Jesus Christ for our salvation.

PREFACE

On September 11, 2001 we saw something awful. We saw sin and evil at its highest possible magnitude. It was an act of total lack of dignity and worth of other human beings. The horrendous acts of violence that were committed against the *World Trade Center* and the *Pentagon* were a violation of every civilized moral principled ethical measure.

The majority of the American people polled that the specific people responsible and behind these acts must be brought to justice: a real, honest and legal justice. They were concerned that in an upset environment of anger and pain, a climate of revenge may take over and nothing could be more dramatically opposite to the basic human rights and the Christian teachings of forgiveness to our enemies, because *they know not what they do*. However, forgiveness does not mean that one is freed from the consequences of one's actions, and does not necessarily happen right away, it will take time.

President *George W. Bush* has requested that during the world fight against terrorism we must observe distinction between the people of Islam and the Ideology of the extremist Muslim militants.

As citizens of a nation that stamped on its coins *"In God We Trust"*, we hope and pray that these acts of terror will cause us to look deeply and persistently for clues as to why we are the object of terrorism? Why so many Muslim believers are willing to die in the process of bringing so much pain into our lives? What they are telling us? And what are we saying in return?

I was born and raised Christian in a Muslim dominated country of Egypt, I could not stop thinking about the outrageous tragedy and heinous acts perpetrated against the United States. I felt that I am obligated to share what I had learned about Islam with the majority of my fellow Americans, knowing that they are very poorly informed, and as a result they are puzzled, confused and continue to ask why do they hate us?

A principal objective of this book is to contribute to better understanding the other for achieving more safer and peaceful life. It is also an object of this book to inspire active involvement with courage and wisdom to participate in a noble quest of better humanity.

Understanding and learning what Islam is about, its beliefs and its ideology require our concerted mutual efforts to learn and to discover new ways, change attitudes, policies and keep not doing the same things without learning.

Many books are published and articles are written, some by Muslim scholars defending Islam as a religion of peace, and some authored by Muslim people who lived in Muslim dominated countries telling their powerful and often disturbing stories. Some of them were born Muslims, in strict Muslim families. They bring witness to the violence and terror that they escaped when they discovered what is wrong with Islam. When they expressed their opinions and concerns, close members of their own families, Muslim clergy and governmental authorities persecuted them. They explain the dark forces at work in their native countries and bring witness to the violence and terror they escaped.

No one knows how to diffuse an intensifying conflict that Muslim extremists have initiated and continued to confuse the modern world. They simply believe and advertise that Islam is the true way and the only solution for the world's troubles. The conflict and fight between secular and militant Muslims are shaping in today's Middle East and has no end in sight.

Although the underdeveloped Radical Islamic groups are no match to the much more advanced Western world, many Muslim radical organizations are blindly driven by its 1400 year old religious idea that Islam must prevail to rule the whole world. This idea is simply unrealistic but is supported in many Islamic countries. The idea is as comical as the idea of the movie "*The Mouse That Roared*". In 1958, the great British Comedian *Peter Sellers* starred in a very funny movie called "*The Mouse that Roared*" that involves a fictional tiny nation that is financially broke. The little nation decides to declare war on the United States in order to lose the war and then receive vast sums of money in form of international aid from the Americans."

Little by little the Muslim Arabs acted in the same manner of the mouse that roared, they summoned up the psychological nerve to intimate confrontations with the bullies of the west. Today some of these small nations have significant clout on the world scene, including control of energy resources, voting rights or similar status in the United Nations, status in the world community, and more. Many of these third world small sovereign states became breeding grounds for the terrorism as we have witnessed it in the recent years.

Like a mouse that roared, they are either very ignorant to aggravate a sleeping giant or they are very smart calling for America to come, to shut them down, and then give them treat, aid, money, food, and provide them with protection.

Radical Muslims are a small fraction of the whole Muslim world. They believe that they are the true Muslim believers; they do not tolerate any deviation from the teachings of the Quran and the traditions of The Prophet Mohammad. Their goal is Islam must prevail and rule the world. *Radical Muslims* consider secular or moderate Muslims as well as all non- Muslims being nonbelievers and they have declared holy war (*Jihad*) against them.

Although Islam denies God's love to mankind and rejects His salvation in the person of Jesus Christ, I can say that there is a bright side to Islam's ideology that is harmonious with the Jewish and Christian teachings, namely believing in one God the almighty, creator of heaven and earth and every thing therein.

If you are intrigued, then take the opportunity for some great reading in this book "*The Turning Point- Islam and Jesus' Salvation*", pray for God's help and ask that He reveals himself to you through His Holy Spirit to enable you recognize and accept Jesus Christ who gave his life for forgiveness of our sins and for our free salvation to eternal life.

PART I

HISTORY OF ISLAM

Part I contains Seven Chapters; the first two chapters take you 1400 years into history and bring you back in time. The remaining chapters explore the different beliefs of Muslims, their Holy places, culture, economics and art.

Chapter 1. Pre-Islamic Era

Chapter 2. Rise of Islam

Chapter 3. Sects of Islam

Chapter 4. Holy Places of Islam

Chapter 5. Culture of Islam

Chapter 6. Economies of Islam

Chapter 7. Art Work of Islam

1

PRE-ISLAMIC ERA

In the century before the start of Islam, The Arabian peninsula was the scene of collapse and economic decline that co-incited with the decay and fall of the Roman Empire and rise of wars between Persia and the Christian Byzantine empires which controlled Turkey, Syria, Egypt, and North Africa. Conflicts among the tribes of Arabia during this period are known as the *Jahilliah* that means the age of barbarism. In the *Jahilliah*, Bedouins worshipped star gods, sacred stones and idols made by hands. Their highest loyalty was to the tribe or clan groups claiming descent from a common ancestor. Their greatest achievement was an oral literature, poetry of extraordinary quality, claimed as a "high speech" which was recited by the tribesmen to celebrate the deeds of the tribes and heroes.

Pre-Islamic Arabia was hot, dry, barren and rigid land inhabited mainly by nomadic Bedouin tribes who worshiped idols carved from stone sand and pieces of wood supposedly inhabited by supernatural powers. Human virtues by their standards were courage, manliness, loyalty, and generosity. The chief Arabian city was prosperous Mecca, the hub of the lucrative camel caravan trade and site of the *Kaabah*, Arabia's holiest shrine. Chief deity of the city was *Allah*, creator of the universe but still only one of some 300 gods.

Among the sedentary people were of the tribe of *Quraysh*, who inhabited the well-watered rocky valley of *Mecca* and had come to control relatively prosperous sacrosanct territory that other tribes feared to attack. Its little temple, "the *Kaabah*" *is* sacred to the shadowy deity "*Allah*", (*Allah*, cognate with the Aramaic word Allah, the God). *Quraysh* had successfully raised the *Kaabah* to the position of an Arabian pantheon in which other idol gods were worshiped. The people of many Arab tribes came on pilgrimage by camel caravans to *Mecca* to worship and to trade.

By the time *Muhammad* was born around 570 A.D., the influence of both Judaism and Christianity were experienced even in the inner areas of *Arabia*. A general notion of a supreme and sovereign deity seems to have been held by Arabs, and some were identifying God of the Jews and the Christians with *Allah* the God of the *Kaabah*. *Muhammad* was an orphan from a *Quraysh's* clan called *Hashim* that had a record of opposition to the *Quraysh's* leading clan *Umayyad* who had concentrated wealth in their control and exploited their tribal brethren.

It is said that Muhammad was raised illiterate, unable to read or write and most of his fellow tribal people were illiterate and ignorant of science. The only way for science and culture transfers was through camel trade caravans that traveled to and from more civilized and advanced territories similar to *Syria*, *Iraq*, *Persia*, *Egypt* and *Yemen*.

In the *pre-Islamic* period between 70 and 630 A.D., the Arab peninsula had many Jewish and Christian tribes. *Muhammad* was raised in a very confusing period during which the Jews and the Christians were in deep differences. The Christians were divided into many sects and beliefs. The outcome of the conferences of early churches was the driving force to discriminate against Christian sects that did not believe that *Jesus Christ* is the Son of God, born from the *Virgin Mary* by the *Holy Spirit*, crucified, died and rose from death on the third day. The deity of Jesus Christ, the belief of his oneness with God the Father and the Holy Spirit was debated and disputed by many Christian sects.

In 325 A.D., the *Council of Nicene* was convened by the Christian *Emperor Constantine* to resolve a theological dispute started by an Alexandrian priest called *Arius* about the nature of Christ that spread through out the people. The council led to the formulation of the creed of faith also known as the *Nicene Creed*. The creed, which is now recited through out the Christian world, was based largely on the teaching put forth by a *Coptic* deacon who eventually would become *Saint Athanasius* the Apostolic of Alexandria, the chief opponent of *Arius*.

In 381 A.D., the *Council of Ephesus* was called to discuss another theological dispute occurred over the teachings of *Nestor*, a Patriarch of *Constantinople* who taught that God the Word was not hypostatically or being the substance or essential nature of a person, joint with human nature, but rather dwelt in the man Jesus. As consequence of this, he denied that the person of Jesus to be called Son of God and the Virgin Mary to be called the mother of God, declaring her instead to be called "the mother of Christ". The *council of Ephesus* confirmed the divine nature of Jesus Christ that he was conceived of the Holy Spirit, Son of the heavenly Father, three natures of one indivisible God.

In 451 A.D., the *Byzantine Emperor Marcianus* who interfered with matters regarding the faith of the church called the *Council of Chalcedon*. The council declared that Jesus Christ was of two separate natures, one of a human nature and the other of divine nature, but the divine nature took over the human nature like a drop of water that disappears in the vast ocean. Many Christian churches that were under the rule of the *Byzantine Empire* mainly the Eastern Orthodox churches of *Greek, Egypt, Syria, Armenia, Russia* and others rejected the council declaration. This dispute caused confusion that led to a split caused that the Bishops leading the one universal church to separate into two divisions, namely the Western *Roman Catholic Church* on one side and the *Eastern Orthodox* Churches on the other side who reconfirmed the declaration of the *Council of Nicene*. This rift continued until 1992 when a council of the two families of the churches was held in *Geneva, Switzerland* in which the two sides agreed to the human and divine natures of Jesus Christ are of one essence as declared by the creed of Nicene.

Almost 250 years before *Muhammad's* time and for a period of more than 125 years, exactly between 325 and 451 A.D., the church was struggling to define the Christian faith, this period was very confusing to many people and caused drift of many Christians to many sects that accept the human nature of Jesus as man and Prophet and deny his divine nature as God. This is exactly what *Muhammad* has learned, understood and preached to the illiterate Bedouin tribal people who do not know any better, declaring that he received God's revelations that Jesus is only a man Prophet who was sent by the will of *Allah*.

Illustration of Muhammad praying at the Kaabah.

Muhammad preached that there is no God except *Allah* and that he is the messenger of *Allah*. Muhammad's preaching angered the wealthy and powerful tribe chiefs of *Quraysh* in *Mecca*. They tried to kill him, but he fled for his life to the oasis of *Yathrib*, his birthplace, which later called *Medina* "city of the Prophet". The year 622 A.D. was later marked as the first year of the Islamic calendar (*Hijra*).

"By the time Muhammad was born around 570 A.D., the in.fluence of both Judaism and Christianity was experienced even in the inner areas of Arabia. A general notion of a supreme and sovereign deity seems to have been held by Arabs, and some were identifying God of the Jews and the Christians with Allah the God of the Kaabah."

2

RISE OF ISLAM

Beginning in the Arabian Peninsula in 622 A.D., in little more than a century, the Islamic faith spread east to the borders of China and west to North Africa and the Iberian Peninsula, an area greater than the Roman Empire at its height.

Islam was a new growing monotheistic faith with its roots deep in Judaism and Christianity. Early as 620 A.D., Islam began its modern era. In the following years, *Muhammad* and his few followers faced rejection by people of their own clan; he eventually drew followers of about thirty-nine that later grew fast to seventy. At that time *Mecca* had no powerful central religion, the idols in the *Kaabah* were the focus and the attraction for the pilgrims and for the *Meccas* to meet and get involved in bazaar and trade activities, but devoted little energy to religion. *Muhammad*, on the other hand, was fervent in his beliefs and had represented a threat to the order of *Mecca*.

In year 622 A.D., *Muhammad* claimed that Archangel *Gabriel* took him for a *night journey* up to envision the throne of God in the seventh heaven, where God greeted him, prayed upon him and crowned him to be the last messenger to the world. Then Archangel *Gabriel* carried him into a journey down to *Jerusalem* then back to

Mecca during the same night. After hearing this story, the leaders of the strong tribe of *Quraysh* asked *Muhammad* to preach no more for his God and against their idol gods of *Kaabah*.

To compromise with pagans of Mecca, *Muhammad* made concessions to reason with them by accepting the deity the three dominant idols of pagan goddesses, *Al-lat*, *Menat* and *Al-Uzza*. He ranked them greatest after *Allah* with divine intercession. But the chiefs of Mecca pressed after him and tried to kill him. *Muhammad* then realized that it is time to escape. He flee with his followers from *Mecca* to *Yathrib*, a desert oasis located approximately 200 miles Northeast of Mecca, known now as the city of *Medina*, sending them in small groups and taking a circuitous route to avoid assassination.

A painting depicts Muhammad (top, veiled) and his first four Caliphs, original in the Austrian National Library. (Osterreichische National Bibliothek) in Vienna.

The Turning Point Islam and Jesus' Salvation

To earn acceptance and support of the strong Jewish tribes of Yathrib, Muhammad had revealed *Allah's* revelation that the Jews together with the Christians are believers and he called them "*the people of the book*"; i.e. the people of the Torah and the Bible.

During the following years while Muhammad lived in *Yathrib*, he gained trust of its tribes and the number of his followers increased. *Muhammad* then became more powerful and commanded his followers in raids attacking camel trading caravans that traveled on the desert route from the east leading to *Mecca*. This was the beginning of a new era for *Muhammad*, the military commander.

A 20th century painting showing Muhammad (on the right) being comforted by his uncle Abu- Talib as they hide from the Mecca's during their flight to Medina, Shriner's Hall, Maine.

During the life of the Prophet *Muhammad*, in less than ten years of fighting, Islam spread into the Bedouin tribal territories to cover the entire *Arab peninsula*. Upon the death of the Prophet Muhammad, "*Abu Bakr*" became the first *Caliph* who ruled for two years then succeeded by *Omar* who was the ruling second *Caliph* for a decade, during his rule, Islam spread east and west into the Persian Empire, Syria and Egypt. "*Uthman*" the third Caliph, succeeded Omar and ruled for twelve years during which time the Islamic expansion continued. *Ali-Ibn-AbuTalib* followed Uthman as the fourth Caliph. After *Ali* the *Umayyad Caliphate* was established in 661 A.D. and lasted for about a century. During this time *Damascus* became the capital of Islamic world.

The *Abbasids*, who succeeded the *Umayyad*, shifted the capital to *Baghdad* that ruled for over 500 years. The *Abbasid Caliphate* ended when the *Mongols* captured *Baghdad* in 1258 A.D. The Mongols devastated the Eastern land of Islam and ruled from the *Sinai* desert to *India* for a century, but later they converted to Islam. They were succeeded by *Timor* and his descendents who made *Samarqand* their capital and ruled from 1369 to 1500 A.D. A number of powerful dynasties such as the *Fatimids*, *Ayyubids* and *Mamluks* held power in Egypt, Syria and Palestine were followed by the *Ottoman* Empire that conquered and captured Constantinople and put an end to the *Byzantine Empire* in 1453 A.D.

The *Ottomans* conquered much of Eastern Europe and nearly the whole of the Arab world. The power of *Ottomans* began to fade in the 17th century with the rise of Western European and later Russia. They were later completely defeated in the First World War by the Western nations. Soon thereafter in 1924 *Kamal Attaturk* gained power in *Turkey*, abolished the six centuries of the *Ottomans* rule and established the modern Turkey. *Attaturk* was and remained the only leader in the

Islamic world who established a secular ruling that separates the state and religion institutions in an Islamic Country.

The rise and expansion of Islam after the death of the Prophet *Muhammad* was almost in direct proportion to the decline of the Roman Empire, spreading inexorably from an obscure, remote Roman province practically throughout the Middle East, North Africa and Central Asia. Rise and expansion of Islam continued for a period of almost one thousand years. During the same period the Church of Rome grew even stronger, Western agricultural methods improved and the vital horse collar was invented, while the sea-worthy Viking ships that could sail the stormy Atlantic became the design of choice. Westerner sailors dared to cross the Atlantic to a new World that Columbus had discovered. Clashes between the Western and Islamic cultures were fueled with fear, doubt, confusion and strife.

For over twelve centuries, the relations between Islam and Christianity have ranged from distrust and fear to open warfare; the Muslim conquest of Spain and invasion of France, the Crusades and the Christian liberation of Spain are only a few of the major conflicts.

Politics and economics caused more alienation and hostility between the two cultures.

Two questions between the Middle Eastern Arab Muslim intellectuals are:

Why had the once ever victorious Islamic Empire been vanquished by the despised Christian enemy?

How could they restore their previous dominance?

Since the 13th century A.D., the Muslims suffered defeat after defeat, and the Christian European forces having liberated their own lands and pursued their former invaders whence they had come in Asia and Africa.

In the 17th Century A.D., the rapid and innovative technological and economic expansion of the Western European industrial revolution and the ocean going cargo ships marked the new era both in war and commerce. The free market rules, co-operation and competitions strengthened the commerce and increased the international trade.

By the 18th century A.D., the traditional Middle Eastern products such as coffee, tea and sugar were being grown in the new western colonies in both Asia and the Americas and exported to the Middle East by western merchants. The failure of the *Islamic* empire to meet the technological challenges of the western cultures was paralleled by a growing Muslim dissatisfaction with the state of religious, social and political institutions.

For most historians, the conventional beginning of modern history in the Middle East dates to the year 1798, the time when the French General *Napoleon Bonaparte* landed in *Egypt*. In just three short years he drove out the Muslim *Mamluk's* rule out of *Egypt*, and replaced the Islamic laws (*Shariha*) with a new civil law taken directly from the French laws. The French occupation of *Egypt* lasted for three short years and was followed by an English occupation that continued until its independence in 1952 A.D.

Although the military occupation of *Egypt*, as well as most of the Muslim countries in the Middle East and North Africa, has shocked the Muslims, the direct interface of the Muslims with much more technologically advanced Westerners had opened a window that contributed to their advancement.

During the 19th century, the political collapse of the Western imperialism and internal religious reforms continued to press onto the Muslim people. In the later half of the 20th century the political independence was won by most of the Muslim countries. The accommodation of the Islamic community to modernity and the question of how much of the religious tradition is necessary in recreating the purity of the original religious commitment have continued to exercise the best energies of Muslims. So in the 20th century, Islam as a social unity appeared to be in confusion, but as a system of faith, Islam continued to be vital and expanding.

During the 20th century, the fast industrial and technological advancements of the west widened the gap of wealth and power between the Christian dominated western countries and the Muslim dominated eastern countries. Muslims were left behind while the westerns were achieving new discoveries and reforming their way of life.

The combination of low productivity, high birth rate, and rapidly growing population in the Middle East, provided the correct formula for an unstable and frustrated society. Reports published by the United Nations, the World Bank and other independent research institutions; indicate that the Arab countries continue to move backward behind the west. The contrast with the west and now with the Far East countries is even more disconcerting. In earlier times such discrepancies were not as obvious to notice by the vast mass of the population.

Today, the recent achievements and advancements in the public media, information and communications technologies, even the poorest and the most ignorant are informed and aware of the differences between themselves and others both at the personal as well as the community levels.

Now, the people of the Muslim Countries are increasingly aware of the deep and widening gap between the opportunities of the free world and the appalling privation and repression within them. In view of the high unemployment, living below poverty levels ruled by the one party dictatorship, many Muslims look for a cure by drifting into religion searching for comfort and hope, falling in the hands of the fanatic clergies who believe into illusion that Islam is the only solution for the society chronic problems.

❧

"During the life of the prophet Muhammad, in less than ten years of fighting, Islam spread into the Bedouin Tribal territories to cover the entire Arab peninsula, the rise and expansion of Islam was in direct proportion to the decline of the Roman Empire. Spreading throughout the Middle East, North Africa and Central Asia.

❧

3

SECTS OF ISLAM

Islam became a major world religion, which was promulgated by the Prophet *Muhammad* in Arabia in the 7th century A.D. The Arabic term *Islam* literally means "Surrender" and points to the fundamental religious idea that a Muslim believer is someone who submits to the will of *Allah* through the book of *Quran*, revealed to his Messenger *Muhammad*.

The *Sunnis* and the *Shi'ites* are the two important surviving sects in *Islam*. The *Sunni* Muslims follow the example set by the Prophet *Muhammad* that consolidated the majority of Muslims in the context of the well-defined way of *Allah*. The limits set up in the Quran and the *Ahadith* (sayings of the Prophet), separate the peripheral or sideway positions of the secularists who by definition must be erroneous.

The basic belief of the Muslim *Sunnis* is pronounced by the confession (*Shihadah*) of faith "*there is no God but Allah and Muhammad is the Prophet of Allah*". This fundamental and doctrine of *Sunnis* separated them from other sects of Islam who are viewed as protestors and rebellions of Islam.

Despite the notion of a unified and consolidated community, as taught by the Prophet *Muhammad,* violent differences arose among Muslims within few years after his death. During the reign of the third *Caliph* (deputy or successor of Muhammad) *"Uthman",* certain circles in Iraq accused the *Caliph* of misrule, and the resulting discontent led to his assassination. The rebels then recognized *"Ali",* the Prophet's cousin and son-in-law as the ruler (the fourth Caliph), but later deserted and fought against him. The *Shi'ites* (Party of *Ali*) owe their origin to the hostility against *Ali,* and after his death, the *Shi'ites* demanded the restoration of the rule to *Ali's* family and from that demand developed the *Shi'ite* legitimism to form a new sect of Islam and to start a social reform. Gradually, the *Shi'ites* developed a theological content for its political stand influenced by Gnostic and Old Iranian cultures. The *Imam* (the leader) a figure of political ruler was defined and transformed into a metaphysical supreme being that holds a manifestation of God and the primordial light that sustains the universe and bestows true knowledge on man. Through the *Imam* alone the hidden knowledge and true meaning of the *Quran* revelation can be known, because the Imam alone is infallible, who will return toward the end of time to fill the world with truth and justice.

Thus, whereas the *Sunnis* believe in the consensus of the community as source of guidance and workable knowledge for the Muslim to follow the true way of *Allah,* the *Shiites* believe that this knowledge is derived from useless fallible sources and that the sure and true knowledge can come only through the guidance of the infallible *Imam.*

Perhaps the greatest difference between the *Shi'ite's* Islam and the *Sunni's* Islam is that the *Shi'ite's* Islam introduced the passion motive of worship, which is conspicuously absent from the *Sunni's* Islam. The violent death in 680 A.D. of *Ali's* son, *Hussayn,* at the hands of the *Sunni's* troops is celebrated every year with moving orations, passion plays and processions in which the participants, in a state of emotional frenzy, beat their breasts with heavy chains and sharp instruments, inflicting wounds on their bodies.

Another sect of Islam is the *Sufism,* which adapts spiritual purity and stressed Muslim qualities of moral motivation, conviction against worldly matters and "the state of heart" as opposed to legalist formulations of Islam. *Sufis* reject Quran verses that refer to violence and adapts mystical techniques and believe that they have a privileged inner knowledge that is a way for sainthood. They believe *Sufism* is a true spiritual state, obtains knowledge directly from God, and the concept of *Sufism* is beyond and inaccessible to intellectual penetration. This kind of sainthood ideology posed a threat to the Muslim theologians, who never accepted this form of Islamic teaching as having objective validity.

Ishmaelis is another sect of *Shiite's* that is less extreme, their teachings spread during the 9th century from North Africa to Sind. *Aga Khan* heads the *Ishmaelis.* In their theology they rejected most of the extreme elements and heterodox ideas and believe that the Prophet *Muhammad* is followed by *seven Imams* who interpret the will of God to man and are in this sense ranked higher than the Prophet because they drew their knowledge directly from God and not from the Angel *Gabriel* whom the *Sunnis* believe revealed the *Quran* to *Muhammad.*

Other minor sect of Islam are the *Ahmadis* that started in India in the latter half of the 19th century by a self proclaimed Prophet called *Mirza Ghulam Ahmed.* His teaching adapted certain doctrines, namely that Jesus died a natural death and was not assumed into heaven as the Islamic *Sunnis* believe, and that Jihad "by the sword" had been *abrogated* (cancelled and replaced) with Jihad of the pen. His aim appears to have been to synthesize all Indian religions under Islam. He declared himself to be not only the manifestation of the prophet

Muhammad, but also the Second Advent of Jesus, as well as *Krsna* for the *Hindus*.

Other minor Shi'ites sects include the *Bahais*, the *Yazidis*, and the *Druzes*. There are also many minor sects that are characterized with distinctive features of political and religious motives, similar to the *Asharians, Azzrzgites, Babakites, Babbis, Idrisites, Assassins, Kharjites* and many more.

"Despite the notion of a unified and consolidated community, as taught by the Prophet Muhammad, violent differences arose among Muslims within few years after his death. Muslims are divided in many sects, some seem to have a cult type ideology that stretches into the past of Muhammad's time mentality saying that they are the true believers and that they will prevail to rule the world"

4

HOLY PLACES OF ISLAM

The *Kaabah* sanctuary in *Mecca* is the most holy place for Muslims; it is the object of annual pilgrimage, and is believed to be the place where *Allah's* power touches the earth directly. According to the Muslim tradition, Abraham originally built the *Kaabah* as a copy of and directly below God's throne in heaven. The structure was destroyed during a great flood leaving behind nothing but the foundation. In pre-Islam era The Kaabah was used as a shrine for pagan idols, especially *Al-Lat, Menat and Al-Uzza,* known together as "Daughters of God" and *Hubal,* a God of marriage. When Muhammad took control of Mecca, he destroyed the idols and dedicated the Kaabah to Allah.

Painting of Muhammad re-dedicating the black stone at Kaabah, from a Manuscript in the Library of the University of Edinburgh, illustrated in Tabiz, Persia, 1315 A.D.

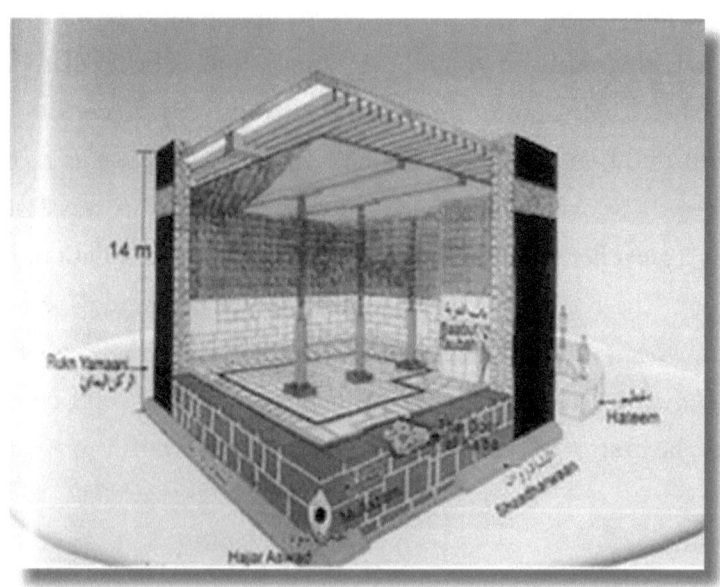

Illustration shows the interior construction of the Kaabah. The Sacred Black Stone is located in the corner and three wooden pillars support the roof structure.

The structure of the Kaabah measures 40 feet long, 33 feet wide and 50 feet high. The Kaabah is built from gray granite and each corner points to one of the compass directions. The single entrance is on the northeast side approximately 8 feet above ground. The interior of the Kaabah is bare except for three supporting wooden pillars and gold hanging lamps. Affixed to the eastern corner about 5 feet is a sacred black stone.

Photo of the Kaabah building during the
annual change of the cover (kiswa).

The exterior of the Kaabah is usually covered with a large black cloth called the "*Kiswa*" or a robe decorated with Quranic verses embroidered with gold thread. Each year a new cover is tailored, and until 1927 it was provided by an Egyptian artesian who brought it with them in pilgrimage camel caravan that traveled across the desert land from Cairo to Mecca.

Muhammad flying over Mecca, at the beginning of the "Night Journey" The Square building in the center is the Kaabah, from a manuscript currently in the British Museum.

Recent Photo of Muslims Pilgrims Praying at Al–Kaabah.

The Prophet's mosque in *Medina* is the next in sanctity. Medina is the birthplace of the Prophet Muhammad; it provided sanctuary for him to escape persecution that he faced in Mecca.

Jerusalem follows in third place in sanctity as the first *Quibla* (the direction to which Muslims face when praying). Muhammad changed this later by receiving a Quran revelation to face the Kaabah. According to the Quran, Jerusalem is the place from where Muhammad made his descent from heaven to earth, the *Dome of the Rock Mosque* was built after the Muslims invaded Jerusalem to mark the spot where they believed Muhammad has touched earth upon his return from his *Night Journey*. This spot is said to be over the remains of the *Great Temple of Solomon.*

Many other holy shrine places are located in the Muslim countries around the world constitute places of special veneration to the Muslim people.

Illustration of Dome of the Rock, and Al-Acssa Mosques in Jerusalem, the second most holy place for Muslims, built over the great temple of Solomon site in 650A.D. Muslims believe this is the place Muhammad visited during his Night Journey to heavens.

Dome of the Rock Mosque in Jerusalem.

A photo of the Prophet Muhammad's Mosque in Medina.

❧

"The Kaabahisapre-Islamicstructure,Muhammad re-dictated it. According to the Islamic traditions, Abraham originally built the Kaabah, and it is the place where Allah's power touches the earth directly."

❧

5

CULTURE OF ISLAM

The early Islamic culture is founded and built on foundations established by prior civilizations of countries that were invaded and occupied by Muslims. Islamic culture was a synthesis of Byzantine, Greek, Syrian, Persian, Indian, Egyptian and Spanish cultures. It digested as well as borrowed virtually every field of human endeavor, most significantly in medicine, astronomy, navigation mathematics, art, architecture and construction.

Hagia Sophia Church in Istanbul Converted by Muslims to a Mosque.

Hagia Sophia is a Greek name meaning "Church of the Holy Wisdom of God." It was built in 537 A.D. at the orders of Emperor Justinn and was converted to a mosque in 1453 A.D. under the Islamic rule of the Ottmans. In 1935, by the orders of Turkish leader *Kamal Attaturk*, Hagia Sophia was turned into a museum. After the building conversion to a mosque in 1453 and due to the Islamic ban on imagery, many of its mosaics Christian icons were destroyed or covered with plaster.

Uncovered mosaic icon of Christ as Master of the World
(Panocrator) on the dome of the Hagia Sophia.

Photo of Granada Great Mosque in Cordoba.

After the Arab conquest of Cordoba of Spain in the 7th century, Granada became a vibrant trade link between the west and the Muslim world. Granada is now one of the most famous tourist cultural spots that mark the Muslim and Christian historical legacy.

By the second half of the 15th century, the Christian monarchs of Spain forced the predominantly Muslim population to leave the land to Northern Africa. The mosques, some of them were former Christian churches were converted back to Christian uses. Part of the Muslim population converted to Roman Catholicism.

The expelling of the Muslims from Spain in 1542 ended the eight hundred year-long Islamic presence, freed Spain from conflicts with Muslims and led to a united Spain that was to become the Spanish Empire that embarked the greatest phase of expansion around the globe, leading to the discovery of the Americas in the first half of the 16th century.

Islamic civilization reached its high point during the 10th century as a kind of Middle Eastern renaissance. The culturally backward Arabs contributed little to civilization and humanity just not more than the Arabic language, but that in their opinion was the decisive factor. Arabic language of the *Quran* was a great unifier of the faith, just as Latin was once a common language of the Church of Rome. The Arabic form of writing was also important, leading to Islamic art of the development of an infinite variety of abstract ornament and remarkable system of linear abstraction that is uniquely Islamic. Art of architecture designs were distinctive achievements that were not of particular people, culture or country. Unified and shaped by religion, Islamic art and architecture were among the glories of an entire civilization.

Artifacts were discovered all over the world for civilizations in the period between 3000 years B.C. and the birth of Islam, but no significant artifacts are found for *pre-Islamic* civilization in the Arab peninsula. Muslims take claim of the artwork related to arabesques, geometric motifs and interface patterns that was developed in Persia, Syria, Egypt, Byzantine (Turkey), and Greek.

It is well known that Islamic traditions prohibit the presentation of human beings and animal images as art objects; however, this order was not observed by secular artists, they developed paintings and images of *Muhammad* himself.

Islam discouraged writing of books that contain writings outside the context of the *Quran*. It is known that Arab Muslims are accused of burning and destructing the famous great library of Alexandria. The Arab worriers under the leadership of *Omar Ibn-Al-Ass* entered Egypt in 642 A.D., when he reached the city of Alexandria; he found a huge library building that contained tens of thousands of books and records. He sent a massage to the *Caliph* describing his finding and asking for guidance. After three months, the *Caliph's* strict order came: "If these books contain what is in the book of the *Quran*, we do not need them, and if they contain any writings different from what came in the *Quran*, they are not from *Allah* so burn the books". *Omar Ibn-Al-Ass* set fire in the great library of Alexandria,

It is said that the fire consumed the library that housed records of ancient civilizations from the time of the Pharos that were collected over a period of 1000 years, namely around 350 B.C. the time of Alexander the Great to the time of the Arab invasion in 641 A.D. It is known that the library and school of Alexandria was an important center and source of knowledge to the world of that era.

Central to the Muslim's life is the Prophet Muhammad and the *Caliphs* (his successors) whom continued his message and teachings. The person of Muhammad encompassed the secular and sacred, but for the Muslims both are one and the same. During his life, the Prophet was simultaneously the embodiment of Islamic law (*Shariah*) and the chief priest, his duties varied from settling legal disputes to leading the people in prayers or as a chief commander in fights that sustained all the Arabian Peninsula.

Later, Islamic civil unrest and rebellion among local authorities led to weakening of the central power system of the *Caliphates*, and the Muslim society became much less autocratic.

During the modern times, and in response to attacks from the West, the Muslim empire was reduced and disintegrated to a group of separated countries ruled by rebel chiefs; the majority of them assumed life time reign and had complete unlimited power.

Political instabilities in the Middle East opened the way for the West to assume control and rule almost all the territories that were under the rule of the late great Islamic empire. This led to establishing new democratic governments and constitutions that were adopted from the West. In Egypt, *Napoleon Bonaparte,* the French General, conquered and expelled the extreme Muslim Mamluk's regime and established a new constitution based on the French civil law for the Egyptian judicial system that replaced the Islamic law (*Shariha*). Similar changes took place in India, Pakistan, Iran, Turkey, Libya, Morocco, and Algiers,

However, after World War II and after achieving their independence, many of these countries fell again in the hands of the Islamic extremists who were supported by the windfall of wealth from huge petroleum discoveries. The Islamic ruled *Saudi Arabia* led the way to re-establishing the Islamic Empire under the *Wahhabi* Islamic ideology throughout the Middle East. The *Wahhabi* Ideology follows the literal teachings and enforces the Islamic rules set by the Prophet Mohammad in the *Quran* and the *Ahadith.*

After the 911 terrorist attacks on the United States, President George W. Bush said that he will see to it to root out the extreme Muslim terrorists and that the military invasion of Afghanistan is the first step to reform the fanatic and dictatorship regime and to establish a democratic model for modern Middle East. His vision is to stop the extreme Muslims aggression and to reform and enrich the lives of the people in these countries.

"The early Islamic civilization is founded and built on foundations and advancements achieved by prior civilizations of countries that were invaded by the Muslims. Islamic culture was a synthesis of Byzantine, Greek, Syrian, Persian, Indian, Egyptian and Spanish Cultures."

ↅ

6

ECONOMIES OF ISLAM

Since the 17th century, the western countries grew rich and powerful, while the Muslim-dominated Middle Eastern and Far Eastern countries have fallen behind in wealth and power. The technology advancements that continued through the present time has reduced and marginalized the role of religion in political and public life in the western Christian dominated world.

On the contrary, most of the Muslim dominated countries have fallen in the hands of the religious clergy and *Mullahs* to run their societies. Turkey is the only Muslim country that embraced the goal to separate its state and religion institutions. Governments of other countries similar to Egypt, Jordan and Bahrain has recently took initiatives and started to realize and take such steps to reform and face the real cause of their economic troubles, namely in Islam there is no separation between state and religion institutions.

Islam is a way of life where religion and state are indivisible and cannot be separated. What has been revealed in the book of *Quran* and the sayings of the Prophet *Muhammad* that are recorded in the book of "*Ahadith*," control a Muslim's life and behavior. Islam offers a simplistic solution to socialism; however socialism is not a packaged deal that can be obtained from a book as revealed in the *Quran*.

The poor and hungry millions in many Muslim countries would rather have the basic needs of food, cloth, shelter, etc. With exception of the recently enriched oil producing countries namely *Saudi Arabia, Bahrain, Qatar, and Arab Emirates*, the majority of the Muslim countries became impoverished and continue to get poorer. The vast majority of their Muslim populations live under the minimum poverty levels with no hope insight.

Just recently, Muslim leaders and economists woke up to the reality that the ideology of the indivisible religion and state of Islam is to be blamed for the cause of the Muslims poverty and misery. The cure is not achievable as no one has the courage to suggest or to cross the limits line to prevent changes or reforming what came in Quran established by *Allah* and his prophet, the result is communities that are confused, troubled and in conflict with its dictatorship type rulers. In their confusion they search for ways to be accepted into today's modern and secular countries where the church and the state are separate institutions.

It is not just poverty, illiteracy, and the absence of commonly accepted moral standards; it is rather the increasing awareness among educated Muslims that they have failed as a civil society of being able to confront the real causes of their economic problems.

For over fourteen centuries, the inherited pride of Muslims and their self- serving political agenda has long blinded them, so they became unable to accept the other, and reduced Islam to organized state sponsored hypocrisy that is supported by the ruling parties and only benefit their dictatorship cause.

Available economic and social reports published by the United Nations and World Bank for the Muslim developing countries provide important indicators for the state of economy and the development of the Islamic world. Published data similar to high rate of population increases, low life expectancy, low number of physicians per capita, high illiteracy rate and low gross domestic production (GDP) per capita, are indicators of poor quality of life and chronic economic and social troubles that plague the Muslim population.

The lack of urban and city planning combined with alarming high rates of population increases combined with the deteriorating infrastructures are critical obstacles to the economic development. In addition these countries rely heavily on services provided by local governments for major public transportation, communication, information management, energy and utilities all of which lack capacity essential for physical distribution of goods and services.

Other indicators, similar to low per capita steel consumption, cement production, electricity production, and domestic water usage correlates with the troubled economic state of the Muslim dominated societies.

As a result, the Muslim population became valuable customers and users of the Western research, products and services. As customers they seek the latest cutting edge technologies, standards and procedures; however they have no proven track record to materially invent or to contribute to the development of new products or more advanced technologies.

Many Muslim scientists became more creative, some became inventors and famous when they left their homelands and fled to healthier and free Western World where they could improve their quality of life and where the freedom of religion does not restrict their way of thinking.

"It is not just poverty, illiteracy, and absence of commonly accepted moral standards; it is rather the increasing awareness among educated Muslims that they have failed as a civil society not being able to confront the real causes of their economic problems."

7

ARTWORK
OF ISLAM

Throughout the history of mankind, art has been considered the most important measure of advancement of civilization for a society and its people. Islam began in Arabia in the 7th century A.D. Prior to the Islamic era, there is no known original Arabian art work found except linguistic Arabic poetry that is referred to the pre-Islam and early Islam period. The term Islamic art denotes art works produced from the 7th century onwards by the people (not necessarily Muslims) who lived in the territory that was inhabited by culturally advanced populations lived under the Islamic rule.

In the first four hundred years after Muhammad, Islam made remarkable expansion through a series of disruptive barbarian invasions, first by tribal groups, and then by hostile armies formed of new converts marched under the flag of Islam. They focused on exploiting or even destroying existing civilizations they encountered. During the early period of spread of Islam, the less advanced Arabs encountered more advanced cultures; it took Islam several centuries to absorb the non Islamic cultural, artistic, social, and ethical aspects into a single coherent cultural unit, creating much different combination of aspects of Islamic Art for an empire stretching from Spain to central Asia and Northern India. Islam continually engaged in an anxious soul searching in the new societies.

Muhammad's Ahadith (sayings) and traditions display a deep distrust of pictures, this led to a difficult balance between religious toughness, flexible creative and human advancement. To the picture makers He said: "On *the Day of Judgment, the most terrible of punishments will be in.flicted on the painter.*" He instructed his companions not to paint a picture of him, and this has been taken as a general prohibition and blanket ban condemning images of any kind, he also told them not to pray in places that have images. Images of people or animals are generally forbidden, artwork is restricted and reduced to only flatter space figures connecting geometric design lines, objects, floral patterns and illustrated Arabic word motifs of the names of Allah, and of verses from the Quran.

There has been few known sculptures of Muhammad, a stamped image of the Prophet's head on a medallion was carried by the Elite of the Ottoman's army, one statue of Muhammad can be seen on the face of the building of the U.S. Supreme Court where Prophet is honored by the Artist as one of the great "law givers" of mankind.

The growing power of Islamic extremists strengthened the old ban on depictions of the Prophet. So did the rise of the *Wahhabi's* in *Saudi Arabia*, their conservatism went as far that they obliterated the Prophet tomb as they feared veneration. Until recent times, many Muslims have felt some hesitance about permitting portraits of any kind, not so long ago some Saudis died a violent death while attempting to prevent television with all its images from entering their land, now millions of the Saudis watch it every day!

Abundance of monumental architecture and architectural decorations exhibited in mosques, arches and cathedral designs are borrowed from the Byzantine and Spanish.

The old Islamic ban on *depictions of the Prophet* is frequently ignored by Muslims, as these many paintings and hand made books of history were seldom authorized to legitimize one or another Islamic dynasty. In the era of the *Caliphs*, the *Sultans* and the *Shahs*; the period between the early 13th and late 17th centuries; numerous great Islamic paintings and artwork were commissioned, many of these old paintings of the Prophet are on display in public institutions in *Istanbul, Vienna, Edinburgh, London, Dublin, Los Angeles and New York*. Four are in Washington D.C. in the Smithsonian Freers's Museum. Old portrayals of Muhammad come from Sunni lands and Shiite ones, from Turkey of the Ottomans, India, Mongols, Uzbekistan, Afghanistan, Syria and Iran. The oldest that survived were painted in circa 1300, the newest were produced about 200 years ago.

Pictorial representations of the Prophet are widely available; they remain accepted by many Shi'ites although most Sunnis have generally forbid them. These elegant and fine artistic paintings were once Imperial luxuries, and kept in costly buildings, the rulers who commissioned them were attempting to ally themselves with God-approved courageous figures of the past, the painters produced them carefully and piously with respect to portray the documented life, teachings, battles, triumphal events of the Prophet and his Caliphs. Manuscript illuminations picturing Muhammad that survived are on display in the Metropolitan Museum of Art in New York, the British Museum in London and the Freer in Washington, D.C., all tell historical and cultural facts about Islam's past times.

Many of those old Paintings portray Muhammad's claims about Heaven, Hell, and the last Day of Judgment. One of those, is the *Night Journey*, a Persian painting (1556-1562), has been 60 Years among the prized possessions of the Smithsonian's Gallery art collection. It is touched with gold painting, we see the Prophet in the sky, and winged angels fly around him, surrounded with curly and vague clouds. Muhammad isn't floating; He is riding a Buraq; a wondrous supernatural human-headed horse that carried him in a single night from Mecca to the seven heavens. The Buraq's coat is spotted and his hat is trimmed in fur. The Prophet's face is hidden, but the golden aura that surrounds him shows just who he is.

The Night Journey, a Persian painting (1556-1562),
Smithsonian's Gallery Art Collection, Smithsonian's
Art Museum, Washington D.C., USA

Artistic paintings of Arabian dancers

⁓

"Images of people or animals are generally forbidden in Islam, Permitting artwork is restricted to only .flatter space Jigures connecting geometric design lines and objects, .floral patterns and illustrated Arabic word motifs of the names of Allah, and verses from the Quran."

⁓

PART II

IDEOLOGY OF ISLAM

Part II contains nine chapters covering the life of the Prophet Muhammad, his teachings, the book of the Quran and the ideals that form the basis of Ideology of Islam.

8

THE PROPHET MOHAMMAD

Muhammad was born around 570 A.D. into the family of *Hashim* of the Powerful tribe of *Quraysh*. Muhammad's father *Abdullah* died before his birth, his mother *Amina* died when he was six years old, he also lost his grandfather *Abdul Muttalib* who took care of him since his birth.

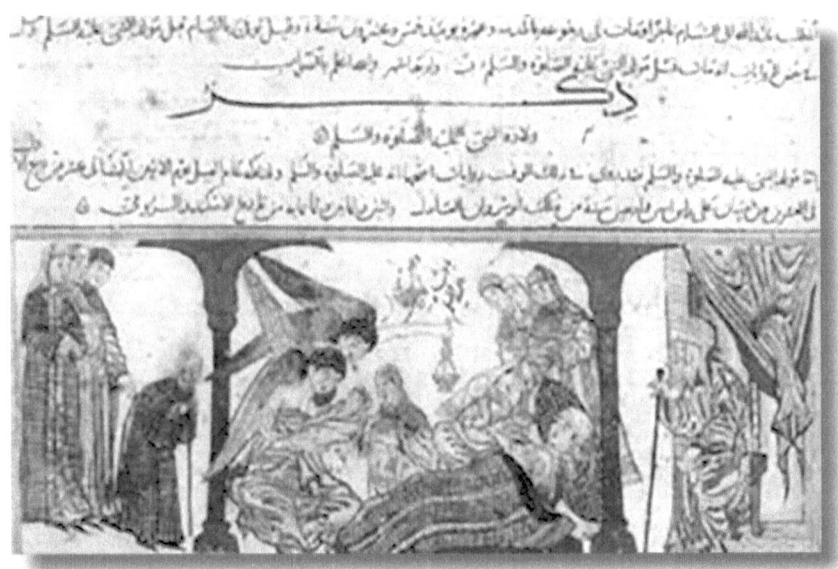

Illustration of the Birth of the Prophet Muhammad, Tapriz, Persia, 1315A.D. In The Library of the University of Endinburggh.

The newly born Muhammad in his mother's arms being shown to his grandfather and Meccans, from Turkish book illustration, University of California, San Diego. (Date unknown)

Muhammad was then put under the care of his uncle *Abu Talib*. In his childhood Muhammad had to earn his own livelihood by serving as a shepherd boy and trader. When he became twelve years old, his uncle *Abu Talib* took him into trade camel caravan missions to Syria. In the desert route to Syria, there was a Christian monk named *Buhaira*, who lived in solute in an outlaying mountain cave. In his way to Syria and until his return, *Abu Talib* used to leave young Muhammad in the care of the monk *Buhaira*.

Buhaira followed the teachings of *Nestor, Nestor* was a Christian Bishop and then a Patriarch of Constantinople, he denied the deity of Jesus, rejected the holy trinity, believed that Jesus was just a prophet, and that he was not crucified nor died on the cross.

In the Holy Church Council of *Ephesus* in 431 A.D., *Nestor's* teachings were rejected and he was ex-communicated, released from his Church leadership responsibilities and was exiled into southern Egypt. Muhammad learned the heresy of *Nestor* and it became the centerpiece of his thinking, he learned from *Buhaira* some Jewish and Christian teachings.

It is said that Muhammad was illiterate, cannot read nor write, so the monk taught him to recite in a chanting rhythm the stories of creation, Adam and eave, Noah, Lot, Isaac, Ishmael, Jacob, David, Solomon, Joseph, Moses, Aaron, Zechariah, John, Mary, Jesus and many other biblical stories.

Muhammad as a youth meets monk Buhaira, Tabriz, Persia,
315 A.D., the library of the University of Edinburgh.

Muhammad in his youth was known to be sincere, honest and faithful. At age of twenty-five, after a successful trade caravans to Syria for a wealthy widow by the name of *Khadija*, she was 15 years older than him, from the respected tribe of *Quraysh*, uncle *Waraqa Bin Nofel* was a Christian Bishop of Arabia who followed *Nestor's* teachings, he blessed their marriage; Muhammad married *Khadija* according to her Christian faith prior to his claim of receiving the Quran revelation from the Angel *Gabriel*, they lived happily together and she was his only wife until her death in 620 A.D.

Muhammad's call to prophesy on the first revelation, 1425 A.D., Harat, Afghanistan, the Metropolitan Museum of Art.

It was undoubtedly that during his travels on many business trips, he had encountered Judaism and Christianity.

After *Ibin Nofel's* death and when Muhammad was about 42 years old, he began his practice of retiring to a mountain cave to mediate and claimed that he had seen visions of an angel. *Muhammad* began preaching in *Mecca* to his entrusted inner circle and friends. His ministry was basically monotheistic made up mostly of Jewish and Christian teachings that he learned since his childhood.

Later when *Muhammad* became 52 years old, he claimed that God revealed and spoke to him through the Angel *Gabriel,* who instructed Muhammad to recite the words of Allah. The revelations happened over a period of ten years. *Muhammad* recitation of Gabriel's words was recorded later by his followers and grouped in 114 chapters (*Surahs*), which are collected in the Islam's Holy book known as the *Quran*.

Muhammad gradually started to preach his believes, attracted a small minority mostly his wife *Khadija*, his uncle *Abu-Talib*, and several relatives and friends. The majority of the more powerful and influential members of the tribe of *Quraysh* and those of smaller clans of Jewish and Christian faith opposed this new self-proclaimed prophet.

Arab illustration showing Muhammad (on right) preaching to the earliesvt converts. From a manuscript in the collection of the Bibliotheque Nationale, Paris. (Munuscrits Arabe 1489 fol.5v).

The opposition to Muhammad grew from intolerance to hostility and persecution against him and his followers. However, Muhammad's life was protected by virtue of his relation to his rich and influential uncle *Abu-Talib* and the family of his wealthy wife *Khadija*. At the beginning, Muhammad's rejection was limited to social, verbal abuse, harassment and threats. On the religious level the powerful *Mecca's* resisted Muhammad's doctrine of *Allah's* oneness since it went against their belief in the power of their idol Gods and Goddesses. On an economical level, he was a great threat to the financial stability and the richness that the nobles of *Quraysh* earned year after year from the busy season of pilgrimage. Every year thousands of people traveled into caravans from other countries as far as India, Persia, Syria, and Yemen to worship their favorite idol Gods and to trade in Mecca.

In order to ease the tension and to win the support of the aristocrats of Mecca, Muhammad proclaimed deities of *Quraysh's* favored three stone Idol Goddesses, *Al-lat, Mennat* and *Al-Uzza* who had high status among the *Meccas*, he proclaimed that Allah revealed to him that these three idols are divine beings whose intercession and effectual with Allah. Muhammad's recognition of the idol Goddesses was short lived, it became obvious that his mission is not succeeding in Mecca.

After the death of his beloved wife *Khadija* and his uncle *Abu-Talib,* he married a widow of one of his followers; he then married *Ayisha* who was just nine years old, daughter of his close friend *Abu-Baker.* In summer of 622 A.D., he and few of his followers flee Mecca to take refuge in the near- by Oasis of *Yathrib*. *Yathrib* is about two hundred miles north of *Mecca*, known now as *Medina*, the city of the Prophet. This act of refuge is known as the *Hijra* (Immigration); it was so significant to mark the start of the beginning of the Muslim's year.

*A glass painting from Singal showing Mecca's searching
to capture Muhammad who was hiding in a Cave
during his flight to Medina in 622A.D.*

Muhammad later denounced his previous Quran verses of the divine deities of the three Idol Goddesses, he said that he was tricked and deceived by Satan, the verses have become known to the modern biographers as the

"*Satanic Verses*", some took it as an evidence that Muhammad was just a human being like any other man, he was tempted by Satan.

Muhammad revealed to his followers that Angel Gabriel took him on the back of a heavenly creature having a face of an angel and a body of a horse with wings (*Buraq*), into a *Night Journey* to visit the heavens, where he met with all the previous prophets, Moses, Noah, Abraham, Jesus, etc. Gabriel accompanied him to see the gardens and virgins of the paradise. Finally took him into the presence of Allah where he received specific instructions for the Islamic rituals of worship and prayers. The mystical story led to increased hostility against Muhammad and many of his followers began to doubt his right state of mind and his truth fullness.

Scene of Muhammad riding Buraq during the night Journey.

*Muhammad meets the prophets Ishmael, Isaac, and Lot in
Paradise, from Apocalypse of Muhammad, 1436 A.D., Hatat,
Afghanistan, (Currently in the Bibliotheque Nationale, Paris.)*

In *Yathrib (Medina)*, Muhammad and his followers were accepted, primary by native tribal people inclined more toward monotheism, their strong cultural influenced by several well established Jewish tribes in the area. Natives of *Yathrib* (Medina) had heard from the Jews that a prophet was soon to appear in the region; therefore, they were eager to accept Muhammad as that anticipated prophet whom to come and claimed him for their own. In *Yathrib* Muhammad was welcomed, he became a leader and married several times after his third wife *Ayisha* keeping thirteen wives of his own at the same time.

However, Muhammad tried but failed to win support of *Yathrib's* three large Jewish clans, although he made some concessions in order to find favor with the Jews, such as he commanded his followers to turn to the direction of Jerusalem when praying and he adopted the Jewish Day of Atonement and the midday prayers time as established in Jerusalem. The Jews rejected Muhammad's message and his claim of prophet-hood, because of many discrepancies between his Quran revelations and their own sacred scriptures.

During the second year in *Yathrib*, and under Muhammad's command, few of his followers started to raid against camel trade caravans that traveled the route between Mecca and Syria. The first raid was carried out successfully; they killed the merchantmen, looted the merchandise and the camels, and took the women and children into slavery. The victory led to attract more armed men to join Muhammad's worriers who continued to attack more trade caravans.

The Prophet Muhammad riding a camel surrounded by his companions during their flight from Mecca to Medina (Hijra), a leaf from a copy of the Majmac al-tawarikh (Compendium of Histories), 1425 A.D., Timurid. Harat, Afghanistan. In Metropolitan Museum of art.

In 624, with 350 of his armed men, Muhammad attacked a large camel trade caravan coming from Mecca, which was guarded and protected by over one thousand armed men. Muhammad's men ambushed the caravan and defeated the Mecca's army at a place called *Bader.* They divided the spoils and Muhammad kept one fifth of every thing. Muhammad's victory at Bader assured him that Allah was on his side.

After the battle of Bader, Muhammad and his followers terrorized the region and made several attacks on the Jewish tribes who previously rejected him in Medina, among these tribes were *Banu Qaynuqa, Banu*

Nadir and Banu Quraizah all of them suffered great losses, Muhammad's followers massacred over one thousand Jewish men, their women and children were sold into slavery and their property was divided among Muhammad's followers.

Muhammad receives revelations from Angel Gabriel during a battle. (Source unknown)

After several attacks on camel trade caravans, the route to Mecca became risky and dangerous for travel. The trade between Mecca and the east had to come to a stop. Mecca's economy suffered and the city became under siege.

In the year 628 A.D., the sixth year of *Hijra*, a treaty was made between the elders of the *Quraysh* tribe in Mecca and Muhammad. Both sides agreed to keep peace for a period of ten years. In return, Muhammad and his followers were allowed to visit Mecca and to make pilgrimages in peace. Two years later Muhammad broke the treaty, attacked Mecca with an army of ten thousand men and took control of the city. He destroyed all the idol gods and executed all those who resisted him.

Muhammad (riding the horse) receiving the submission of The Banu Nadir, a Jewish tribe he defeated at Medina. From Jami'al-Tawarikh, Dated 1315 A.D., Khalili's collection of Islamic art, London.

Muhammad (on the left) leading his followers against Banu Qaynuqa,
a Jewish tribe defeated at Medina, from the Jami'al Tawarikh,
dated A.D.1315. Khalili's collection of Islamic art, London.

Muhammad destroys the idols of Mecca, taken from Manly
P. Hall's occult guide "The secrets Teachings of All Ages"

Upon the conquest of Mecca, Muhammad stood at the zenith of his power. The city that had refused to listen to his mission, mocked him and his followers, driven him and his people into exile, unrelentingly persecuted and boycotted him, this city now lay at his feet. When the city surrendered without fight, Muhammad entered Mecca victoriously and declared pardon to all men who once chased him out of the city. The undisputed political and religious leader of Arabia and Mecca became the center of Islam.

Muhammad sitting on a rug at a banquet with his companions.

In 632 A.D., the tenth year of *Hijra*, Muhammad died and after his death a power struggle ensued among his followers, leading to a division and warfare between the Muslims. Several different sects branched out within Islam. The *Shi'ites* and Sunnis became the two major Muslim branches.

Muhammad face covered lying during his death
surrounded by his close companions and wives.

The sources of Muhammad's biography are numerous, but on the whole untrustworthy, being crowded with fictitious details, legends and myth stories. None of his biographies were compiled during his lifetime, and the earliest was written a century and half after his death. The Quran is perhaps the only reliable source for the leading events in Muhammad's lifetime. His earliest chief biographers are *Ibn Ishaq* (768 A.D.) and *Al- Bukahri* (870 A.D.) collected what is called the *Ahadith* or the sayings and traditions of the Prophet Muhammad, the historical value of which is more than doubtful.

These sayings and traditions in fact represent a gradual and more or less artificial legendary development rather than supplementary historical information. According to them, Muhammad was simple in his habits, but most careful of his personal appearance. He loved perfumes and hated strong drink. Of a highly nervous temperament, though gifted with great powers of Imagination, he was affectionate and magnanimous, pious and austere in practice of his religion, brave, zealous and above reproach in his personal and family conduct. Muhammad is shown by his life and deeds to have been a man of dauntless courage, great generalship, strong patriotism, merciful by nature and quick to forgive, and yet he was ruthless in his dealings with the Jews

Concerning his moral character and sincerity, scholars have expressed contradictory opinions in the last three centuries. Many of these opinions are biased either by an extreme hatred of Islam and its founder, or by an exaggerated admiration coupled with hatred of Judaism and Christianity. Remarking the judgment of these modern scholars, the conclusion and the verdict of history goes against the teachings of Islam and the morals of its founder.

In his book "*Christ, Muhammad and I*": Mohammad Al Ghazoli; a Muslim scholar who came to Christ, wrote: "*As a Muslim, I realized that Islam was not the truth and could not be the truth… it is hard to understand the kind of God that Muhammad claimed that he was His messenger. It is impossible that the true God would encourage killing, destroying, robbing and shedding the blood of the innocent.*"

"Historians have often and hotly debated the continuing significance of the Prophet Muhammad, wondering whether it is military, religious or rather one of cultural impact. In which areas do you think does he belong?"

9

WOMEN OF THE PROPHET

Muhammad's first wife, Khadijah, died at age 69, he was 54 years old. After her death and in the remaining nine years of his life, he married 11 or 13 women depending upon the differing accounts of whom he wed as a wife. Many Muslim scholars imply that Allah exempted Muhammad from the restriction that forbids a man to marry more than four wives at any time. They refer to the Quran's revelation that allowed Muhammad to have many wives according to the following verses providing

to him the legal right to marry whoever he wishes:

"O Prophet! Surely we have made lawful to you, your wives whom you have given their dowries, and those whom right hand possesses out of those whom Allah given to you as prisoners of war, and the daughters of your father's brothers and the daughters of your father's sisters, and the daughters of your mother's brothers, and the daughters of your mother's sisters who fled with you and a believing woman if she gave herself to the

prophet, if the prophet desired to marry her, this is specially for you and not for the (rest of) the believers; We know that we have ordained for them concerning their wives and those whom their right hand possess in order that no blame may attach to you and Allah is Forgiving, Merciful" (Quran 33:50).

The following account of the women of prophet Muhammad is from the Arabic book titled "The Women of the Prophet" authored by Dr. Aisha Abdul Rahman (Bint Al Shati) of Egypt and from the book of "Christ, Mohammad & I" written by Mohammad Al Ghazouly.

- *Khadijah* was the first woman whom Muhammad had married and she was his only wife until she died. She was from a Christian family, her uncle Waraqa Bin Nofel, was then bishop of Arabia, they were married according to her Christian faith. They had two sons who died young, then they had four daughters: Zainab, Ruqaiya, Umm Kulthum and Fatimah.

- Muhammad's second wife (after Khadijah) was *Sawada*, a widow of one of his followers. She was 55 years old, not so beautiful but good hearted, loving and kind person.

- Muhammad married his third wife, *Ayisha*, when she was nine years old. He was fifty-four years old. Ayisha was Muhammad's favorite, when he died at age of sixty-two, Ayisha was only seventeen years old, a young woman at her prime, but she was forbidden to remarry as revealed in the Quran preventing Muhammad's wives from remarriage.

- The fourth marriage of Muhammad was his niece *Zainab*, she was the wife of Zaid; Muhammad's adapted son. One day Muhammad went to visit his adapted son Zaid, when he entered the house, Zaid was not home, and Muhammad saw Zainab half naked, Muhammad desired her and said "praise Allah who changes hearts", Zainab smiled and later told her husband Zaid about Muhammad's statement, Zaid was terrified of Muhammad's lust for his wife. Muhammad himself wanted to have her, but he knows it is wrong and was worried more about how his followers will perceive his desire. Angel Gabriel came to rescue him and revealed that Zaid should divorce Zainab for the prophet to marry her, so it was done in the name of Allah's order. Some would ask how Allah so easily destroy and separate two people in marriage to satisfy

Muhammad's desires and lust? How could Allah who is just and merciful agree to such an atrocity? How could the prophet of Allah lusts after his own adopted son's wife? How could the prophet make it lawful to himself what he made unlawful to the rest of the world? Muhammad even violated the three-month waiting transitional period that is mandated by Allah for a woman to abstain before remarrying again after a divorce from her first husband. He did not observe the traditions and the law that requires having a legal guardian and two witnesses for a marriage to be lawful. When Zainab asked Muhammad about who would be her guardian? And who would be the two witnesses for their marriage? He answered, "Allah is your guardian and Gabriel is our witness." As a result of his statement, Zainab boasted later in front of his other wives saying "Your fathers gave you in marriage but as for me, it is Allah who gave me in marriage to His Messenger." Some Muslim Scholars question Muhammad's state of mind, immoral incursion and behavior when he lusted for Zainab the wife of his adapted son.

So controversial was Muhammad's desire to marry his adopted son's wife, and to his justification with his stern pronouncement on the very institution of adoption, which had tragic consequences to this day. After he married Zainab, Muhammad revealed few verses in the Quran against adoption (Quran 33: 4-5) these verses are widely interpreted to imply that adoption is forbidden in Islam. The result is unknown number of millions of children in the Islamic world have been needlessly orphaned, all because Muhammad's search for a dignified way out to nullify his lustful desires for a married woman of his own adopted son, lust that went beyond what his other six wives (at that time) and unknown number of female slaves could satisfy.

- The fifth marriage for Muhammad was to **Safia**, the daughter of Hayiy, a Jew of the tribe of Khaibar... It was in the seventh year of Hijra (629 A.D.), when Muhammad raided the tribe of Khaibar.

During that raid, many of Khaibar's men were killed and much of their possessions were looted and their women were taken captives. Muhammad ordered her father killed, and her husband tortured until he divulge the hiding place of his money. After he told them, Muhammad ordered him killed and took his wife as a slave. Safia was very beautiful, only seventeen years old, a one-month pride in marriage to her husband who was ordered killed by Muhammad. At that time Muhammad was fifty-nine years old. He married her, deprived all her rights and she had no say regarding what happened to her people and her family. Three years later she became a widow for the second time after the death of Muhammad. But this time she was forbidden to remarry because of Muhammad's revelation from Allah that prevents his wives from remarriage.

- The sixth wife was **Juwayriya**, another Jewish captive, daughter of Al-Harith, the chief of Banu Mustaliq, who were defeated in a battle after a surprise attack. Juwayriya was exceedingly beautiful, twenty years old when Muhammad was fifty-nine.

- **Um Salma** was the seventh wife of Muhammad, she was another beautiful woman, and she was the daughter of the sister of Uthman (the third caliph). When Muhammad saw Um Salma at Uthman's house, he inquired about her, Uthman told him that she is his niece, and her husband is Abdullah… In few days Muhammad ordered her husband to carry the flag at the front in the battle of Uhud, he was wounded and died. The next day Muhammad entered into Um Salma, and thus she became his sixth wife.

So far Muhammad had six wives after Khadijah's death; Swada, Ayisha, Zainab, Safia, Juwayriya and Um Salma. Swada was the only homemaker among the wives of Muhammad; she was the oldest, not so beautiful, but good at heart. One night it was her turn to sleep with him, Muhammad told her of his decision to divorce her; she heard the news with great surprise, and felt as if the walls were falling down on her.

So she begged him saying, "please keep me, O Messenger of Allah". He answered her, I will keep you upon one condition; you would give your appointed night to Ayisha. Swada agreed, saying from now on, I would not desire what women want, for I give my appointed night to Ayisha. As a result, Muhammad kept her as a wife, but visited her no more.

- Muhammad's eighth wife was **Um Habiba**, Ramlah, the daughter of Abu Sayfan, her husband Ubied, rejected Islam and turned back to Christianity after their flight to Ethiopia. After his death, she returned to Arabia and Muhammad married her. Her husband, Ubied was the brother of Zainab (Muhammad's fourth wife), Ubied confronted Muhammad and said to him "You are neither a prophet nor a messenger of Allah, stop claiming that, I am a believer in Christ for He is the truth, but you are a self-conceited man".

- The ninth wife of Muhammad was **Maria the Coptic** (A Christian Egyptian); she was given as a present to Muhammad from the Byzantine ruler of Egypt (Al Muqauques). Muhammad loved Maria and spent more time with her than with his other women. One day she went to see him at the house of his wife Hafsa (the daughter of Omar-the third Caliph), Hafsa was not home at that time, when suddenly she returned home she found Muhammad having intercourse with Maria in her own bed! She exclaimed saying "how come you do this in my own bed and how you do this on my appointed day?" The prophet, whom Allah's revelation came on him, said "Keep this a secret, do not tell any one and do not tell Ayisha". Muhammad trembled with fear continued: " I will not touch Maria again, and I declare to you that your father (Omar) and Ayisha's father (Abu Baker) will rule over my nation after me, I have bequeathed that to them". But Hafsa told Ayisha and his wives started to gossip about what Muhammad had done and that he asked them to keep it a secret. As a result, Muhammad divorced Hafsa, when the news reached her father, Omar, he became very angry and almost left Islam. When Muhammad heard about Omar's reaction, he immediately took Hafsa back saying that Gabriel revealed to him "Hafsa will be your wife on the resurrection day". But in response to his wives gossiping about the affair, Muhammad decided to have nothing to do with his wives for a month. Further, he declared a warning from Allah known in the Quran by the verse of the warning, revoking Muhammad's wives if they continue to give Muhammad trouble, Muhammad to divorce them and Allah will provide him with better wives!

- *Maymuna* was the tenth wife of Muhammad, married her during the pilgrimage (Al-Hajj) journey to Mecca. Despite the fact that Muhammad revealed in the Quran that it is forbidden for Muslims to marry during the pilgrimage month, he took an exception to make his action legal, Angel Gabriel came with a revelation from Allah to allow him to marry Maymuna immediately and without delay, leaving his followers another contradiction that Muhammad persisted on doing all his life.

- The eleventh wife of Muhammad was **Hafsa** daughter of Omar bin Al-Katab, is another woman whom Muhammad married and added her to his list of wives in the third year of Hijra (625 A.D.).

- **Raihanah** was a Jewish captive from the tribe of Bani Quraiza, she became a Muslim and Muhammad kept her as a slave.

- **Asma, Shraaf, Allia and Wasna** were also known to be the wives of Muhammad.

స్త

"Muhammad's wives established an example to the Muslim women to accept an inferior social position, treated as subordinate persons whom must be under the full authority and domination of men, this oppressive condition of women is asserted and authorized through the Quran and Ahadith of the prophet of Islam."

స్త

10

THE BOOK OF QURAN

Muslims believe that Angle Gabriel revealed the Quran to the Prophet Muhammad over a period of 12-years that began about 620 A.D., and continued until his death in 632 A.D.

They believe in the validity of his prophet hood, that his teaching is a divine message directly from Allah and that the message is embodied in the Holy Quran. The Quran is revealed in Arabic language, the living word of Allah to all of humanity. They believe that the earthly Arabic written book, bound between covers, is a copy of eternal book that is kept in heaven.

Eleventh century, North African book of the Quran, in the British museum .

Angel Gabriel appearing to Muhammad at Mount Noor (A hill near Mecca) where Muhammad received his first visions, 18th century, Turkey, currently in the collection of the New York Public Library.

The Quran consists of verses grouped into 114 chapters (*Surahs*). The chapters vary in length from a few verses to over 200 verses. Much of the Quran is written in rhymed Arabic prose. Muslims believe that Arabic is the language of the heavenly Angels and that the rich, forceful language of the text is humanly unmatchable, this by its virtue is a miracle that confirms Muhammad's prophet hood.

The central teaching of the Quran is that there is only one God, known in Arabic as *Allah*. Allah is the creator of the universe. Allah, in his mercy, sent the Quran as a guide for humanity after sending many of his prophets. The Quran mentioned the prophets Abraham, Moses,

Jesus and many others. But Muhammad as the last and the crown of all the prophets.

Angel Gabriel cleansing Muhammad's heart of impurities in preparation for his ascension to heaven, which the other angels watch, 16th century, Turkey.

The Quran speaks of a last day of judgment when people shall stand before Allah to account for their lives. It contains many teachings to regulate Muslim's daily life. It requires daily prayers and stresses charity and brotherhood among Muslims. On one hand, the Quran requires from Muslims to struggle and fight to spread the word of Allah to all nations, on the other hand, it teaches that one should be humble, temperate, brave and just.

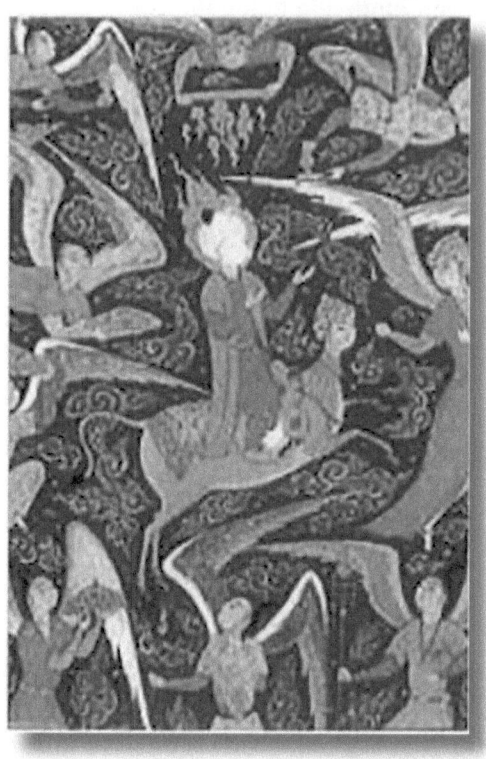

*Ascension of the Prophet Muhammad riding Buraq and surrounded
by angels during the night journey (Source unknown).*

The Quran is the final and highest authority for Islamic laws in all matters and practices for all Muslims. It formed basis of the fast Islamic expansion of the past and it guided and inspired Muslims for over 14 centuries.

The Quran has been taught orally and is memorized, at least in part by virtually all Muslims, even illiterate Muslims possess and prize the text and many of them memorize and recite the entire book by heart. The art of properly reciting the Quran has been preserved and passed through the centuries. For hundreds of years those Muslims, who do not speak the Arabic language, religiously memorize its verses in Arabic words; even they do not fully comprehend what they recite.

Muslims consider translations of the Quran to other languages as only a way to teach Islam to non-Arabic speaking people. They believe that translations do not preserve the words of Allah in their original form and the Quran must be recited in Arabic. Since

Angel Gabriel dictated the Quran to Muhammad in Arabic, Muslims believe that Arabic is the language of the Angels.

The Quran is unique among all known sacred scriptures in teaching a doctrine of *Abrogation* according to which the later pronouncements of the Prophet abrogate, i.e. declare null and void, his earlier pronouncements. The importance of knowing which abrogate others has given rise to the Quran methodology known as "*Nasikh wa Mansukh*" i.e. the "*Abrogators* and *Abrogated*". Because of the changing circumstances in Muhammad's lifetime, various early revealed verses have been cancelled and replaced "*abrogated*" with later revealed verses.

In the Quran, Allah changed his commandments, so the verses revealed to Muhammad when he was weak, humble, patient and tolerant in Mecca, before the year 622 A.D., has been changed after the year of his *Hijra* to *Medina*. Therefore, Muslims must follow the latest teachings and commandments of the Quran verses. For example, the verses that relate to *Jihad* to force the Jews and Christians into Islam replaces the previous ones, Muslims must ignore the abrogated earlier more peaceful verses and must use the later violent verses that call for violence. All these verses were revealed in the last two years of Muhammad's life before his death in 632 A.D.

Scholars who compared the chronological order of the historical events in the Bible with that mentioned in the Quran, found them very scrambled and inaccurate. Many of the so-called prophets in the Quran are not even mentioned or existed in the Old or the New Testament versions of the Bible.

Examples of contradictions between the Quran and the Bible addressing the same stories are:

- *Mary* the mother of Jesus in the Quran is confused with *Miriam, the sister of Moses and Aaron*; she is called as the daughter of *Umran* (Quran 3; 31-37 and 19:28). The Bible tells that she is the daughter of *Joachim,* (Time line difference of more than 1475 years between Moses and Jesus).

- In the story of *Noah*, the Quran reveals that Noah lost one of his sons to the overwhelming floodwater and that the Ark rested on mount *Judi* (Quran 32:48). The Bible tells that Noah, his sons, his wife and his son's wives, all of them went into the Ark and were saved from the waters of the flood and that the Ark rested on the mountain of *Ararat*.

- In the story of Abraham, the Quran reveals that Abraham took *Ishmael*; his older son from *Hagar* his maiden, to be sacrificed. The Bible said that Abraham took Isaac; his son from *Sarah* his wife, to be sacrificed.

- In the story of Abraham, the Quran reveals that Abraham send Hagar and his son Ishmael to dwell in the rigid and dry valley of Mecca, he prayed to Allah that they receive favor and compassion from the people they may encounter (Quran 14:37). The Bible said that Abraham dwelt in *Hebron* and built an Alter to the Lord, He sent Hagar and Ishmael away in the desert of Beersheba (Sinai desert).

- In the story of Moses, The Quran reveals that the wife of Pharaoh took baby Moses to adopt him as a son (Quran 28:8-9). In the Bible, the daughter of Pharaoh was the one who adopted Moses as a son.

- In the story of the *John the Baptist*, the Quran refers to him as *Yehya* and that because his father *Zechariah* doubted and did not believe Allah's promise that he will have a son at old age, Zechariah was punished to be mute for three nights. The Bible tells that he was muted and not able to speak until the child was born, which is the entire period of his wife's pregnancy.

- The Quran refers to Jesus as *Isa,* and reveals that when he was a child he created a bird from clay and let it fly. The Quran reveals briefly that he healed those who were born blind, healed the lepers and raised the dead all by Allah's order and will. The Bible has no mention of the bird story, but recorded in much detail the miracles that Jesus performed and manifested his Glory as the Lord and that his disciples had witnessed these miracles and believed in him.

The Quran describes in much detail the joys and glories of the *paradise* as being fantastic and sensual as the lascivious Arabian nights legendary stories and as the mind could possibly imagine.

A paradise with plenty of water is one of the greatest additions to the delights of Bedouins in a rigid, hot and dry desert land, the Quran often speaks of the rivers of paradise as principal ornament thereof, some of these streams flow with water, some with wine and others with honey, besides many other lesser springs and fountains of camphor and musk, their earth consists of pebbles of rubies and emeralds, their sides of saffron.

Resplendent and ravishing girls or *Houris* of paradise, the enjoyment of whose company will be the principal felicity of the faithful, will eclipse all these glories. These maidens are created not of clay, as the case of mortal women, but of pure musk, and are free from all natural impurities, defects, and inconveniences. They will be beautiful, modest and secluded from public view in pavilion of hollow pearls; only the faithful *martyrs* whom die in jihad in sake of Allah will interface with them.

The pleasures of paradise will be so over whelming; Allah will give each martyr the sexual drive and potentialities of a hundred individuals, to each individual a large mansion will be assigned, and the very meanest will have at his disposal at least 80,000 servants and 72 virgins of the maidens of paradise. While eating they will be waited on by 300 attendants, the food will be served in dishes of gold, where of 300 dishes shall be set before him at once, each containing a different kind of food, and an inexhaustible supply of wine and liquors.

The magnificence of the garments and gems is conformable to the delicacy of their diet, they will be clothed in the richest silks and brocades adorned with bracelets of gold and silver, and crowns set with pearls. They will make use of silken carpets, couches, and pillows. In order to enjoy all these pleasures, Allah will grant them perpetual youth, beauty and vigor. Music and singing will also be ravishing and ever lasting.

One of the most popular modern arguments for Quranic inspirations is its scientific inaccuracy, for instance Muhammad revealed in the Quran and Ahadith the following scientific claims:

- Allah created the *stars* for three purposes: decoration in the sky, signs to guide travelers and as missiles used by angels to shoot demons.

- Human *embryos* go through a blood clot stage.

- People used to be very tall (90 feet).

- The *sun* rotates around the earth and sets in a pool of murky water.

- *Ants* can talk.

- *Allah's throne* is over waters.

Muhammad's view of reproduction of human beings is terribly flawed. Muhammad believed that a man's semen is produced between the ribs and backbone and that a woman produces a similar substance. A child's appearance is based upon which of the parent's discharge is secreted first during their sexual intercourse. He also believed that the sperm-stage lasts for forty days, that the developing embryo becomes a clot of blood, and that the child's gender is determined more than a month after fertilization.

While Muslim apologetics ignore the embarrassing inaccuracies and argue that no way an illiterate, seventh-century Bedouin could have revealed such scientific insights without Gods help and that this is the absolute proof of his status as a prophet and the divine authority of his message. The tactic of a Muslim apologetic's continuing arguments is achieved through the following four steps:

- He reads a simple verse from the Quran or Hadith (Muhammad saying).

- He twists and stretches their interpretation as far as his imagination will take them.

- He inserts a bunch of modern scientific terminology in the interpretation.

- Finally, he proclaims that Allah had revealed these scientific insights to his messenger centuries before the modern scientists have lately discovered them.

After hearing such arguments, Muslims typically stand in awe; others stand there wondering, "Where the simple verse did say that?" However, an honest investigator's only reasonable option is to conclude that Muhammad's supposed scientific precision is notorious for being singularly unimpressive to any one, and that Muhammad's words are not inspired by God, and such errors that are revealed in the Quran can not be the words of God.

The Quran and Ahadith are the main sources of varieties of Islamic mythical and legendary stories:

- The world was created by Allah's word "Be", so it was done (*Kun- fa- Ykun*) out of nothing.

- After the creation of angelic beings from light, Adam was formed from clay and destined to be Allah's vicegerent (*Caliph*). All of the angels obeyed Allah's order to prostrate themselves before Adam, except Satan (*Iblis*), who refused and was cursed.

- Due to Satan's instigation, Adam ate the forbidden fruit and was driven out of the Paradise. Questions of the original sin and Eve's role do not rise.

- Angels and genies (*jinns*) are living powers that become visible in human life; they are accepted as fully real.

- Every human being's destiny is written on a well-preserved tablet in heaven, a change in destiny is not possible.

- The central event in human life is death and resurrection in the last day. Two terrible angels will question the dead; only the souls of martyrs go straight to paradise.

- A messianic figure will appear in the last days (*a Shi'ite's belief*) sometime identified by Jesus. The *Mahdi* will slay the one eyed evil spirit (*Dajjal*) and combat the dangerous enemies *Goog and Magoog* who will come from the north of the earth.

- The trumpet of one of the four angels (*Israfil*), will awaken the dead in the day of resurrection. The day in which all people will be called for judgment, each according to his written record of deeds.

- Angels use balances or scales to weigh the recorded books (an ancient Egyptian idea) to determine destiny of the humans to be sent to Hell or to Paradise.

- A man, who is setup for Hell fire, walks on a narrow bridge that is said to be sharper than a hair (an ancient Persian idea).

The dreadful angels of Hell and horrors of that place are thoroughly described.

- The pleasures of Paradise, with its waters and gardens and the Houris who are permanent virgins, filled with every thing beautiful. Those who repeat certain verses and prayer formulas a certain number of times, or do some good deeds, they will win the right to be present in the vision of Allah, who then will be visible like full moon.

- Allah's throne is on the waters. (Quran 11:9).

- Mecca is the navel of the earth, created 2000 years before everything else, and the deluge (flood) did not reach to the Kaabah.

- According to the *Ahadith* (sayings of the Prophet), the world is conceived as a succession of seven heavens and seven earths, and that the earth is on water, on a rock, on the back of a bull, on a fish, on wind, on veil of darkness.

Muhammad, whose only miracle according to his own words was the reciting of the Quran, is credited and praised by Muslims with innumerable miracles and associated with a variety of miraculous occurrences; it is said that:

- His finger split the moon.

- A cooked poisoned meat warned him not to touch it.

- A palm tree trunk sighed to him.

- A gazelle spoke to him.

- He cast no shadow.

- From his perspiration the rose was created.

- His ascension to heaven (*Israh*); that is still celebrated; astride a heavenly miraculous winged horse (*Buraq*) in the company of angel Gabriel, flew through the seven spheres, meeting the previous prophets, until he reached the divine presence of Allah.

Numerous poems were written by Muslims to praise Muhammad's birth and achievements, describing him as the one who precedes creation, his light is pre-eternal and he is the reason for a goal of creation. He became the perfect man, uniting the divine and the human sphere as dawn is between night and day.

❧

"The Quran is the final and highest authority for Islamic laws in all matters and practices for all Muslims, it formed the basis of the fast Islamic expansion of the past, it guided and inspired Muslims for over 14 centuries. The Quran and the Bible are in conflict of each other, both cannot be right, one is true and the other incorrect.

❧

11

THE NIGHT JOURNEY

The *Night Journey* is the 17th Surah in the book of the Quran. it records a very miraculous event. In 620 A.D. two years before *Hijra*, Muhammad claimed that Arch Angel Gabriel aided him on a journey astride the back of a *Buraq:* a heavenly creature having a body of a horse with wings and a face of an angel. He flew from the *Kaabah* in Mecca to Jerusalem and ascended to heavens (*Israh*) then descended to Jerusalem and back to Mecca (*Miraj*) in one *night journey.*

Persian Miniature from the mid 1500's, depicting Muhammad ascending to paradise astride the miraculous horse Buraq surrounded by angles in Islamic Lore, this event called Israh and Miraj or the night Journey.

Muhammad (upper right) visiting Paradise while riding Buraq, accompanied by angel Gabriel (upper left). Below them, riding camels are some of the fabled houris of paradise "the virgins" promised to Muslim martyrs. Persian, 15th century, the Bibliotheque Nationale, Paris.

In heavens, Archangel Gabriel accompanied Muhammad in a tour to see paradise and hell. In paradise he watched the virgins (*Houris*) in the gardens and met all the previous prophets. Finally, angel Gabriel ushered him into the presence of Allah the Great. Allah blessed him and gave him specific instructions and commandments to deliver to his followers on earth.

In the 1st verse of the Surah of the *Night Journey*, Muhammad praised Allah: "*Glory is to Him (Allah) who made His servant (Muhammad) go by night from the Sacred Temple (Kaabah) to the farther Temple (Jerusalem)*".

Allah spoke of Moses as being truly thankful servant of Allah, He warned the *Israelites (Jews)*; because of their transgressions, He would send a formidable army to afflict them and to destroy the Temple. If they transgress again, He had prepared Hell for them, whoever repents, accepts His Messenger (Muhammad), the Quran and do good deeds will be rewarded in the Day of Judgment.

Allah then instructed Muhammad with a number of commandments to guide his followers:

- Do not interfere with the property of orphans except with the best of motives, until they reach maturity.

- Keep your promises; you are accountable for all that you promise.

- Give full measure, and weigh with even scales.

- Do not follow what you do not know, a man's eyes, ears and heart senses shall be closely questioned.

- Do not walk proudly on earth.

- Serve no other deity besides Allah, lest you should be cast into Hell, condemned and rejected.

- Do not serve other Gods besides Allah.

- Show kindness to your parents when they attain old age, treat them with humility and tenderness, and say: "Lord, be Merciful to them, they nursed me when I was an infant". Your lord best knows what is in your hearts.

- Give to near kin their due.

- Do not squander your substance wastefully.

- Be neither miserly nor prodigal.

- You shall not kill your children for cause of need, Allah will provide for them and for you.

- You shall not commit adultery.

- You shall not kill any man whom Allah had forbidden you to kill, ***except for a just cause***. If a man is slain unjustly, his heir shall be entitled to satisfaction. But let him not carry his vengeance too far, for his victim will in turn be assisted and avenged.

- Allah gave warning to people who love their present life and live in comfort, He resolved to destroy their city, if they persist in sin, judgment is irrevocably passed and the city is destroyed. Allah prepared Hell for those who desire life of this world, where they will burn despised and helpless. As for him that desires the life to come (*Hereafter*), he must strive for it and being a true believer, his endeavor shall be rewarded by Allah.

- Allah warned Muhammad that the nonbelievers and the wrongdoers would not accept him and would declare that he

(*Muhammad*) is bewitched. Allah said that He would cast veils over their hearts lest they understand, and make them hard of hearing, when they hear the name of Allah in the Quran; they turn their backs with indignation. They are surely gone astray and cannot find the right path.

- In the Day of Judgment, Allah will summon all people to answer to him, he will show mercy to whomever He wishes, and will punish whomever he pleases. Intercession will not relieve the distress, because all mankind crave for His Mercy and fear His punishment, for your Lord's Punishment is to be feared indeed. Allah seeks to put fear in their hearts, but their wickedness increases.

- Satan will deceive man and has the power over all who follow him, but will not have power over the true believers; Allah will be their all-sufficient guardian. Those who are not thankful, they shall find no help, but Allah takes care of those who pray and forsake Him.

- Allah affirmed His support to Muhammad and warned him not to compromise with the unbelievers who offer other scriptures in His name; else He will incur on him (Muhammad) double the punishment in this life and the life to come.

- Allah said to Muhammad "*If they ask you about the Spirit, say it is from Allah, and He (Allah) knows.*"

- The Quran is revealed with the truth to proclaim the good news and to give warning, it is divided into chapters (*Surahs*), so that you may recite it and glorify your lord. Allah is merciful.

Muhammad ended the Surah of the *Night Journey* (*Israh and Miraj*) denying the deity of Jesus Christ saying: "*Praise be to Allah who has never begotten a Son, who has no partner in His kingdom, who needs none to defend him from humiliation, proclaim His greatness*"

❧

"*In the Day of Judgment, Allah will summon all people to answer to him, he will show mercy to whomever He wishes, and will punish whomever he pleases. Intercession will not relieve the distress, because all mankind crave for His Mercy and fear His punishment, for your Lord's Punishment is to be feared indeed. Allah seeks to put fear in their hearts, but their wickedness increases.*"

❧

12

ISLAMIC VIRTUE
OF LIFE

The Islamic path of virtue through Allah's mercy and encouragement drives the strength of Muslim's belief, giving them hope to live a better life. Following are some of the Islamic virtues for the believers to live a better and happier life on both earth and hereafter.

- Those who believe in Allah and his messenger, they will get all kinds of blessings from heaven and earth (Quran; 3: 96).

- A righteous man is free of sorrow, fear of danger. "*Those who are righteous shall not fear nor shall they grieve.* (Quran; 7: 35)

- A Muslim believer is safe from the enemies. "*But if ye are steadfast and do right, nothing will harm you*". (Quran; 3: 120)

- Allah's protection and help will accompany a believer. "*For Allah is with those who restrain themselves and who do good deeds.*" (Quran; 16: 128)

- A man who fears Allah is promised deliverance, liberation and a way out of his hardships. *"And for who fears Allah prepares a way out"* (Quran; 115:2) *and he provides for him resources that he never could imagine."* (Quran; 115:4)

- Righteous people are successful in their lives and they are chosen servants of Allah. *"For Allah does love the righteous."* (Quran; 9:7)

- A righteous person will be honored in the presence of Allah. *"The most honored of you in the sight of Allah is the most righteous among you."* (Quran; 99:13)

- Allah forgives the sins of the righteous. *"O' who believe and fear Allah and speak with righteous word, Allah purify your acts and forgive your sins."* (Quran; 33:70)

- The righteous will be delivered from evil and the fire of Hell. *"Allah will deliver the righteous to their place in salvation and no evil shall touch them, nor shall they grieve."* (Quran; 36:61)

- The righteous; shall be ushered into paradise and will live in real pleasure. *" As to the righteous they will be in gardens and in happiness"* (Quran; 102:17)

- The righteous; shall be rewarded in this world, and the hereafter, in this world he will have comfort and blessings of Allah, freedom from fear and sorrow, safety from enemies and he will be granted Allah's company and help. In the hereafter he will have peace in grave, and on the Day of Judgment; the accounting of his deeds will be made easy on him. *"Behold, verily on the friends of Allah there is no fear nor shall they grieve.* (Quran; 11:62), *"Allah guards those who believe against evil"* (Quran; 11:63), *" for them they shall be rewarded in their earthly life and in the hereafter"* (Quran; 10:64), *"Allah the greatest is the life giver, helper and councilor to the righteous.*

"Verily we directed the people of the book (Jews and Christians) before you (Muslims) for you to fear Allah." (Quran; 4:13)

- Piety; is the nature of the faithful and success in his reward in the world and hereafter.

- Possibilities of sins; a man is not perfect with all possibilities of mistakes and sins, Satan, the declared enemy of man works to deceive and divert man away from the righteous way, so he cannot be freed from his mistakes and sins. Only prophets were protected and Allah allowed them refuge in Him from all possible influences of Satan and if they commit any thing wrong, they repent and ask for Allah's forgiveness. Allah is attributed himself as the most forgiving.

- Repentance; is the path to forgiveness, Prophet Muhammad teaches his followers *"Fear Allah wherever you are, follow a wrong deed with a good deed that may nullify it"*

- In the Judgment day, Allah will weigh and balance for every man his good and evil deeds, the Quran declares that all deeds are recorded and kept with Allah for the last judgment day. Whomever his good deeds overweigh his wrong deeds will be rewarded in paradise that is prepared for the righteous people, and whomever his wrong deeds overweigh his good deeds he will be sent to Hell. *"Then he whose balance* (of good deeds) *found heavy will be ushered into Paradise to live of good pleasures and satisfaction. He whose balance* (of good deeds) *found light, will have his home in a bottomless pit, it is hell of Jire blazing Jiercely* (Quran 6: 11)

Muhammad Depicted in this painting at the upper right, riding
a camel. The Painting is called "the Day of the Last Judgment",
unsigned, attributed to the artist Mohammed Modabber. Undated
but likely from the 19th century. In the Reza Abbasi museum, Iran.

- Forgiveness of sins; on the Day of Judgment, men will proceed
  in companies sorted out to be shown the deeds that they had
  done during their life on earth. Any one who had done an
  atom's weight of good, he shall see it, and any one who had
  done an atom's weight of evil, he shall see it." Allah through
  His Justice, Sympathy and Mercy toward his servants, He will
  multiply the good deeds and single the wrong deeds and if the
  person repents, Allah will wash it completely and make him
  free from sins.

Muhammad is depicted in the center of this painting with his face covered observing angels using scales for justice. The painting is called "The Day of the last Judgment" signed by artist Mohammad Modabber, from 1897. In the SA'd Abad Cultural collection, reza Abbasi Museum, Iran.

Prophet Muhammad taught his followers the ways for forgiveness, the most important is increased prayers. Allah's messenger explains that during the last third part of every night (before sunrise); Allah descends to the lowest heaven and says, "*Is there any one asking for forgiveness so that I may forgive him?*" The Prophet said "the most superior way of asking for forgiveness from Allah is to pray "O Allah, you are my Lord, no one has the right to be worshiped except you. You created me and I am your slave, I am faithful to your *covenant and your promise*, I seek refuge with you from all evil I done. I so entreat you to forgive my sins, for no one can forgive sins except you" The prophet added, "If one recites this prayer during the day with faith and died the same day, he will become among the people of paradise. Allah conveys the good news in the book of Quran:

"And for those who fear Allah, He prepares a way out for them. And Allah provides for them resources that they never could imagine, and any one puts his trust in Allah, sufficient is Allah for him." (Quran 35:2-3)

- Undertaking Allah's Mercy: The Quran denotes the wisdom of Allah gives continuous guidance and sends his messengers to man. Allah will punish the unbelievers and have mercy to the believers.

In the following verses of the Quran, Allah says:

"O ye who believe, fear Allah and speak the truth, he may make your Conduct perfect and forgive your sins, he that obeys Allah and his apostle has already attained the highest achievement. We offered the trust to the heavens, the earth and the mountains, but they refused to undertake it being afraid thereof, but man undertook it; he was indeed unjust and foolish, that Allah has to punish the hypocrites and the unbelievers, and Allah turn mercy to the believers for Allah is forgiving and most merciful (Quran 70: 73)

"A man is not perfect with all possibilities of mistakes and sins, Satan, the declared enemy of man works to deceive and divert him away from the righteous way, so he cannot be freed from mistakes and sins, but Allah is forgiving and most merciful. In the Judgment day, Allah will weigh and balance for every man his good and evil deeds, the Quran declare that all deeds are recorded and kept with Allah for the last judgment."

13

FIVE PILLARS
OF ISLAM

Early after the death of Prophet Muhammad in 632 A.D., certain rituals of the institutions of Islam were developed to serve as anchoring points of the community's way of life, these are known as the five pillars of Islam: *Faith, Prayer, Zakat, Fasting and Hajj.* Following is a brief definition of each pillar:

- The first pillar of Islam is ***Faith***, a Muslim must profess his faith by saying "*There is no God but Allah and Muhammad is the Prophet of Allah.*" The profession must be recited at least once in one's life time, aloud, clearly and positively with an understanding of its meaning and with an assent from the heart.

- The second pillar of Islam is ***Prayer;*** there are five congregational prayers in a day, although they may be offered individually if one cannot go to a mosque for some reason. The first prayer is at early morning, before sun rise, the second prayer is at noon time, the third prayer is at afternoon, the forth is at sunset time and the fifth prayer is just before retiring to bed. However, only three prayers are mentioned in the Quran: morning, midday and evening. Before praying, ablutions are performed by washing hands, face and feet. The *Mu-azzin*; the person who calls for the prayer; chants aloud from the mosque's minaret (tower). When the prayer starts, the *Imam*, the person who leads the prayer stand in the front facing

Mecca and the congregation stand behind him in rows, repeats after him various prayer parts. Each part consists of recited Quran verses said aloud or silently, at each change of a prayer part, they recite, "Allah is great". Tradition has fixed the verses to be recited in each prayer part. The Friday congregational prayer sermon consists of preaching in local language and reciting verses from the Quran in Arabic. Friday speech has usually considerable impact on public opinion regarding sociopolitical issues. In strict doctrine, the five daily prayers cannot be waived even for the sick that may pray in bed. During travel when water is not available, ablution is stimulated and prayers may be performed without washing with water.

- The third pillar of Islam is **Zakat**, Zakat is the obligatory permanent tax levied by the Quran on every Muslim. The tax is payable annually on grains, cattle, goods, property and cash possessed during one year. The tax rate amount varies for different categories. For example the tax rate on grain and fruits is 10% if produced in a land watered by rain and is reduced to 5% if the land is watered artificially. The tax rate for cash and precious metals is 2½%. Zakat is collectable by the state's Islamic financial institution and to be used primarily for helping the poor, the Quran allows other purposes, such ransoming Muslim war captives, redeeming chronic debts of people, tax collector's fees and Islamic education. After the breakdown of the Islamic Empire to smaller states, Zakat became voluntary charity that depends on the individual conscience. In some countries Zakat is officially collected, but on voluntary bases.

- The fourth pillar of Islam is **Fasting**, Fasting is observed during the month of *Ramadan,* (the ninth month of the Muslim lunar calendar). Fasting begins at daybreak and ends at sunset. During the day, eating, drinking and smoking are forbidden. The Quran states that it is the month of Ramadan that the Quran was revealed. After the Muslims are signaled by the sound of a cannon and hearing the *Muezzins* chanting from the mosques, Muslim families gather around for breaking the fasting, eating whatever they wish and desire. They wake up after midnight to eat another meal before sunrise of the next fasting day. If one was not able to fast during the days of Ramadan, fasting may be postponed until a later time when he becomes able to makeup the missed fasting days with an equal number of fasting days. Instead he may feed a needy person, this is allowed for those who can afford it.

- The Fifth pillar of Islam is **Hajj**, the Hajj is an annual pilgrimage to Mecca prescribed for every Muslim once in a lifetime; provided that one can afford it; and provided that a person has enough provisions to support his family during his absence. The pilgrimage ritual season begins every year on the 7th and ends on the 10th of the month of *Zu-al- hijjah,* (the last month of the Muslim lunar year). About six miles from Mecca, a pilgrim arrives at the limits of *Ihram,* he wears two seamless garments, and neither shaves nor cuts his hair or his nails until the ceremony ends. The rites of Hajj include circling the Kaabah, kissing of the black stone, and going seven times back and forth between the mountains of *Safa and Marwa,* as Abraham's second wife *Hagar* is believed to have done during her search for water. This ritual may take several days and is followed by a group prayer on the *plain of mount Arafat*. During the Hajj, Muslims are forbidden to harm any living being even their enemies, even ants or insects within the Holy site. After the ceremony on mount Arafat, they stay overnight and offer a sacrifice on the last day of Hajj, which is the beginning of the feast day of sacrifice.

An old picture of the Kaabah in Mecca.

"Certain rituals of the institutions of Islam were developed to serve as anchoring points of the community's way of life; these are known as the five pillars of Islam: Faith, Prayer, Zakat, Fasting and Hajj."

14

MORALS AND ETHICS IN ISLAM

Morality is recognizing right from wrong and morals are conscience directives to what to do and what not to do in a society. A person's faith or religion is the main source of his morals, values and ethics that he may adopt during his life. The theological virtue to faith is to secure belief in God and trust in his Prophets, commandments and will. Faith and belief do not rest on logical proof or material evidence and guides a person to accept something without proof, as opposed to believing an idea based on experience.

The previous chapters of Islam's virtue of life and the five pillars of Islam provide many common morals that are observed by other religions and cultures. It would be very easy to point a finger to followers of a certain religion with accusations of wrong doings. For example, Muslims may point to the Christians violent act of crusades against Muslims, but they cannot blame it on Jesus who they believe is whole perfect and holy.

Muslims at large believe that the Prophet Muhammad is the most moral and perfect example of a true Muslim. They believe that he stands as the best model for a man in piety and perfection and that Mohammad is the unique prophet from God. The majority of Muslims believe in what a Muslim scholar describes Muhammad by the following statement:

"Prophet Muhammad is the most favored of mankind, the most honored of all apostles, the prophet of mercy. He is the best of prophets that God send to people, and his nation is the best of nations that God created on earth. He was a perfect intellect and was of a noble origin. He had an absolutely graceful form, complete generosity, perfect bravery, excessive humility, and useful knowledge. Perfect fear of God and had sublime piety. He was the most perfect mankind in every variety of perfection."

The claim of Muhammad's moral perfection has been challenged early during his lifetime and until the present time. The following is a brief outlook of such documented challenges to the teachings of the prophet Mohammad:

Polygamy is sanctioned by Muhammad's Quran revelation. A man is allowed to have up to four wives if he is able to provide for them at the same time. Mohammad revealed to his fellow men *"Marry women of your choice, two, or three, or four"*

It is well known that the Jews and Christians believe in a monogamous marriage relationship between one man and one woman. It is also well known that the majority of Muslims are monogamous. The majority of humankind considers polygamy as morally wrong.

Prophet Mohammad took exceptions for himself from the Quran revelations; he had fourteen wives at one time. He justified his acts to his followers with special revelation from Allah to allow him to marry as many women as he may wish and desire, yet he forbids other men in the Muslim community to have more than four wives at a time. Almost every time Muhammad took a new wife, he proclaimed that Angel Gabriel revealed to him a divine sanction to marry her. To marry *Zainab* the wife of his adapted son; he divorced her from her husband, and added her to his wives as revealed to him by Allah. Muhammad took *Ayisha* a wife, she was a child of just nine years old.

Adultery, a Muslim man and a woman may verbally marry and have sex after they pronounce the words *"I marry myself to you according to the law (Sunnah) of Allah and his apostle"*. Later the man can let the woman to go by just saying to her *"you are divorced"*. Here, they both believe that they have legally complied with the Islamic law and morally they did not commit the sin of adultery. Many Muslim intellectuals classify this sexual act as a legalized prostitution.

Violence is associated with the ideology of Islam. Early when Muhammad was in Mecca, he said that Allah send him as mercy to the world. He later became a military commander terrorizing, attacking; killing and taking plunder to finance his cause and growing territories.

Deceit is an acceptable behavior, Muhammad taught his followers how to be deceitful in order to overcome their enemies. In a Hadith the prophet Mohammad said *"If you cannot conquer your enemy, make peace with him, walk with him in the way, and when he trusts you and retires, get up and kill him."* This is known in Islam as the act of *"Takia."*

Human Rights in Islam are incompatible with the normal civilized rights or constitutional rights that are known in modern times. Following are some examples:

- Men are superior to women (Quran 2:228)
- A Woman has half the rights of man as a witness in court (Quran 2:282) and inheritance (Quran 4:34)
- A man may marry four women at the same time. (Quran 4:3)
- A man can divorce his wife by oral announcement, the wife has no such right. (Quran 2:229)

- Muslims must fight until their opponents submit to Islam. (Quran 9:5)

- A Muslim apostate (person who leaves Islam) must be killed. (Quran 9:12)

- A Muslim must not take a Jew or a Christian for a friend. (Quran 5:41)

- No separation between the state and religion. (Quran 2:193)

- No opposition party is allowed (Quran 4:59)

The Quran and the Prophet's sayings and traditions (*Ahadith*), provides bases for the extreme Muslims to use violence and terror to force non- Muslims (Infidels) into Islam. Suffering of the African Christian natives of *Dahfur* in southern Sudan is an example. This suffering is paralleled with the cooperation of the Islamic ruling regime of the country of Sudan who sponsored tribal Arab militias known as the *Janjaweed*. Terror reigns for cleansing, attacking and *killing* the non-Muslim natives, *stealing* their possessions, kidnapping and *raping* their women and taking the children into *slavery*. Such criminal and terrorist acts are considered legal acts of Jihad to struggle as true Muslims to spread Islam and defeat its enemies. The world International Criminal court had indicted many Sudanese officials who allow these violations to the human rights, causing suffering and displacement of more than two million people and the death of hundreds of thousands in one of the largest genocides in Africa.

It is hardly necessary here to emphasize the fact that ethics of Islam are inferior to those of Judaism and even much more inferior to those of the New Testament. Although in many respects the ethics of Islam are not to be compared with such in Christianity. In Islam there are many ethics that require great deal to admire and to approve beyond dispute, but for originality or superiority there are none. What is really good in Islam's ethics is either previously known or borrowed from some other religions, whereas new added characteristic is nearly always imperfect or wicked.

A painting depicts Muhammad and his companions watching his Nephew Ali bin Abu Talib beheading Nasr bin Al-Harith. Illustrated under the reign of the Ottman ruler Murad III, 1595 A.D.

ରେ

"Muslims at large believe that Prophet Muhammad is the most moral and perfect example of a true Muslim. The claim of Muhammad's moral perfection has been challenged early during his lifetime and until the present."

ରେ

15

WOMEN IN ISLAM

One of the major points in which Islam is criticized by both Muslims and non-Muslims is the treatment of women. Under Islamic laws, women often must remain fully covered, they are denied contact with non- related men, and they can be denied the ability to get jobs and to earn education to the same level as men. Women in Islam have less political and social worth than men and are discriminated against in a variety of ways.

Muslim scholars explain, debate and insist that this is for their women own good, but normally this does not win support.

A true female Muslim believer is required to fully cover her body from head to toe. This was not an order from man, but it is Allah's order and is revealed in the Quran. So extremists believe it is their duty to execute Allah's order to gain favor as obedient believers.

Photo of a muslim woman in full Burga to cover her from head to toe, following Muhammad's revelation for his wives to cover up.

- A Muslim woman's testimony is considered half of man's testimony;

- *"Call in two male witnesses from among you, but if two men cannot be found, then one man and two women whom you judge fit to act as witnesses". (Quran 2: 282).*

- Men are more superior and excel women;

- In a Hadith narrated by *Abu Said Al-Khudri*: The Prophet asked a woman *"Is the witness of a woman equal to half that of a man? The* woman said, "Yes, the Prophet said, "This *is because of the deficiency of the women's mind"*. (Hadith – Bukahri 3:826).

- Muslim females receive less inheritance than males;

- *"Allah charges you concerning supporting your children, to the male the equivalent of the portion of two females, and if there are more than two females then their portion is two-thirds the inheritance, and if there is only one female, then her portion is half* " (Quran, 4:11). *"If a man die childless and he had a sister, her portion is half the inherit age, and he would have inherited from her if she had died childless. If there are two sisters, then theirs are two thirds of the inheritance, and if they are brethren, males and females,* **unto the male is the equivalent of the shares of two females.** *Allah expounded unto you, so that ye err not. Allah is knower of all things."* (Quran 53:27)

Photo of a Muslim woman wearing Hijab

- Men are in charge of women. Women must be obedient to their husbands, and husbands may beat their disobedient wives; "*Men are in charge of women because Allah hath made some of them to excel the other, and because men spend of their property to support them. So good women are obedient, guarding in secret that which Allah hath guarded. As for those (women) from whom ye fear rebellion, admonish them and banish them to beds apart, and scourge them. Then, if they obey you, seek not a way against them; Allah is ever high, exalted, and great.*" (Quran 4:34)

Afghanistan woman in burqa covered head to toe.

- Men are allowed to marry up to four wives, and have sex with slave girls; "*If you fear you cannot treat orphans with fairness, then you may marry other women who seem good to you, two, three, or four of them. But if you fear that you cannot maintain equality among them, marry only one or any slave girls you may own, this will make it easier for you to avoid injustice."* (Quran 4:3).

- A Muslim man can marry a non-Muslim woman, but a Muslim woman cannot marry a non-Muslim man.

- A Man can divorce his wife at any time for his own purpose, just by saying to her; "Go, you are divorced."

- A woman cannot divorce her husband, except if she gives up all her rights.

- An oppressed or abused wife is not allowed to leave her husband's house. If she does, the Islamic laws permits the husband to force his wife to live with him, he may batter her and keep her in suspense until she submits to him.

- If a man divorces his wife three times in a raw, he will not be allowed to remarry her again, except if she get married to another man, then divorced from him. This rule provides a Muslim man the permission to remarry his previous wife after he divorces her three times.

- Allah commands man not to divorce a disobedient wife but keep her in suspense: "*You will not be able to deal equally between your wives as much as you may wish, but turn not them altogether away, leaving her as in suspense, if she do good and keep from evil, Allah is ever Forgiving, Merciful.*" (Quran 4:129)

- A woman is the likeness of a field to be tilted by man; "*Your women are a tilt for you* (to cultivate), *so go to your tilt as ye will*" (Quran 2:223)

- A woman is a sex object, must be protected and covered up. A true Muslim woman cannot be seen by men, except by men of her immediate family members, such as her husband, father or a son. In Islam a woman is thought of as a sex object and must be protected from the eyes and lust of strange men.

Muslim Scholars believe that the Quran and Islamic Laws maintain women's religious and moral equality. With the same token, women in Islam are subordinate to men in their own family and the society as a whole. Some Muslim scholars explain why Muhammad's wives were ordered to totally cover up and to wear the veil or the burga known in the early time of Islam.

According to a Hadith recorded in Sahih Bukahri and narrated after Ayisha, the wife of Muhammad said: "after Hijra from Mecca to Medina, the wives of the prophet used to go at night to an open outlaying open field to answer the nature's call. Omar used to secretly watch them, he used to ask the prophet to order his wives to be veiled, but Allah's apostle ignored him and did not respond to his request. One night, Swada the wife of the prophet went out after dark to answer the nature's call, she was a tall woman and easy to be recognized, in her way back, Omar addressed her saying "I have recognized you O' Swada". He said so knowing that she would tell the prophet. So as he expected eagerly, Muhammad revealed the verses of Al- Hijab (the veil), Allah ordered the prophet's wives to totally cover up so no one can recognize them when they go outside the house".

One may wonder, sheltered toilet facilities are now available for most of the people. Why a Muslim woman must be totally covered up? Why a Muslim woman is required to be covered up in an ugly moving tent or burga. Why the 1400 years old sanction imposed to hide women of Muhammad so they go out to answer nature's call, has continued until today as a sacred tradition? Modern Muslims say that the Quran's verses for the burga dress was specific order for the Prophet's women and should not be enforced on all other women.

A photo of modern Muslim style Hijab (head scarf) dressed young women having a good time in front of 700- year-old Castle of Qaita-Bay, in Alexandria, Egypt; Photo is courtesy of M. G. Kozman.

- Women are subordinates to men; Many Muslim scholars and intellectuals face pressing issues regarding the world demands of human rights and equality for women. They call for freedom of women from bondage of a backward culture and tribal rules and traditions of the 6th century that still control their way of life to keep them subordinates to men.

- An example of the male dominated mentality towards the status of women is demonstrated during a TV broadcasted debate about the importance of the women in a true Islamic community. A strict Muslim intellectual was asked, "What would be the reward of a martyr woman who dies in Jihad?" He answered, "She would be admitted into paradise and she will be rewarded as one of the virgins of paradise (whom a martyr man is promised)!

- In another example; a Saudi Arabian family court ruled to divorce a consenting husband from his wife whom were legally married with children, both were willing to continue their marriage, but the Islamic Saudi court ruled to enforce a divorce against their own will. A tribal rule admits a divorce of a husband from his wife, based on inequity between the man's tribe and the woman's tribe. The woman's tribal chiefs must file a formal claim to the Islamic court.

- According to Muhammad, most of the people in Hell are women.

Muhammad, along with Buraq and Gabriel, visit Hell, and see a demon punishing "shameless women" who had exposed their hair to strangers. For their crime of enticing lust in men, the women are strung up by the hair and burned for eternity, Persia, 15th Century.

Many Muslim scholars believe that Islam's legal sources are in the early stages of a major reform of every possible core text of Islamic laws and a process of rethinking the rights of Muslim women is underway. On the other hand they explain that it is not right to stereotyping all Muslim women to having the same image as those who live under the strict Islamic *Taliban* type rule in Afghanistan, *Wahabbi* rule in Saudi Arabia or other extreme Islamic laws (*Shariah*) applied in many countries in the Arab world. Some critics say that the majority of Muslim women live by the intolerant doctrine adapted in the Islamic law (*Shariah*), others say that women merely are for the pleasure of men at the expense of a 6th century tribal backward culture survival.

Many Muslim women who live in developed modern high class Muslim societies or in the Christian western world assert more rights and privileges, many of them feel sorry for those women who have to wear the *Hijab* or the *Burga*.

જી

"Women in Islam are not equal to Men, Muhammad called them deficient in their mind and faith, they are ungrateful and that most people in hell are women"

જી

16

AHADITH KEYWORDS AND ABSTRACTS

After the death of Prophet Muhammad, early Muslims and followers had collected and compiled his sayings and writings that describe his way of life. Sayings of the Prophet (Ahadith) were collected by people who testified that they heard him speak or saw him act during his life. *Ahadith*, plural of the word Hadith, are thousands of short reports or narratives for sayings and deeds of the Prophet Muhammad, these sayings were collected almost 300 years after his death. One of the six most famous and reliable collections of *Ahadith*, is that of *Al-Bukahri* (died 870 A.D.), which are considered by many Muslims as most authoritative.

It is well known that at the time of *Al-Bukahri*, there were literally thousands of false *Ahadith* (sayings); he sifted through them reducing them to about 7000 and then to 3000 eliminating redundant or alike sayings. Muslim sects are not in agreement of what can be considered as a revelation to be included in the book of Quran and what should be viewed as *Hadith*. (Singular of Ahadith) However, the Muslim Sunnis have accepted the *Ahadith* according to *Al-Bukahri* as the most authoritative as the book of the Quran. The following short list of key words reference only abstracts of the most important and well documented Ahadith and topics within the scope of this book.

Ablution: Sins of the nose, face and mouth are cleansed by Ablution. A Muslim must wash his hands, feet, and sniff water before prayer.

Abrogation: Recent revelations in the Quran's cancel the previous revelations; Allah changed his mind and revised his prior commands.

Adultery: Adulteress woman stoned to death, man lashed.

Alcohol: Alcohol is prohibited.

Allah: No one has seen Allah. Allah's throne is over the water. Allah wants people to sin so they seek his Forgiveness. Allah has 99 names. Allah loves to be praised. Allah commanded Muhammad to burn Mecca's people. Allah curses the Jews.

Alms: A compulsory tax.

Angel: Angels are made of light, have wings, they record the names and times of people arriving to prayers, then listen to the sermon. Angels do not go into a house that has a dog or a picture of a creature.

Animals: Muhammad commanded to always kill: a snake, a speckled crow, a rat, and a voracious dog.

Apostasy: Is a Muslim who rejects Islam and converts to other religion.

Muhammad commands the killing of apostates.

Ascension: Muhammad claimed that Angel Gabriel took him into a *night journey* to heavens.

Ayisha: Muhammad's third wife, He married her when she was a child of nine years of age.

Beard: Muhammad commanded Muslim men to let their beard grow.

Beating: Muhammad said to beat the wives, but not severely, Muslims should not strike each other in the face.

Bell: The bell is a musical instrument of Satan.

Bible: The Bible is a source of many verses, stories and quotes copied to the Quran.

Birth Religion: Muhammad said that all humans are born Muslims. Non- Muslim parents change their children's religion.

Black Stone: A sacred stone that Muhammad carried, kissed and placed as a corner stone in the structure of the *Kaabah*. Muslim pilgrims touch and kiss the stone during the *Hajj* rituals.

Booty: is stealing during war conquest. Muhammad allowed his followers to take booty as a reward to keep them in his army. Muhammad allowed his followers to attack and loot the enemy possessions. Booty is a reward and motivation for staying with Islam.

Bracelets: Muhammad cursed women who try to improve their looks by wearing bracelets.

Breathing: Muhammad said, "Do not breath into a vessel while drinking from it."

Christians: Muhammad said that Allah cursed the Christians because they build churches near the graves; they are the worst people in Allah's sight. Christians are thrown into Hell to make room for

Muslims in Paradise. Christians who reject Muhammad will go to Hell because they worship Jesus.

Compulsion: Muhammad commanded that when people reject to accept Islam, fight them and use force to make Islam superior over others. Non- Muslims must pay *Jyzia* (special tax). The earth belongs to Allah and his Messenger. Become a Muslim and you will be safe.

Curses: Muhammad cursed the Jews and the Christians and those who reject Islam. Muhammad cursed women who wear bracelets and women who are tattooed.

Dead People: Muhammad said that dead people talk, but humans couldn't hear them. The dead can hear you but cannot reply back.

Demons, Demons are chained during the fasting month of *Ramadan*. Demons steal children and utensils. Demons hear angels speak; they repeat and add lies to it.

Dhimmies: Jews and Christians who live in Muslim communities under the rule of Islamic law are called *Dhimmies*. Muslims are not allowed to kill them, but no Muslim should be killed for killing a *Dhimmi*.

Divorce: A Muslim man has the right to divorce his wife at any time just by saying to her "You are divorced". Muhammad commanded that it is better not to divorce a wife, but to keep her in suspense and take another wife.

Dogs: If you keep a dog as a pet in the house, you loose reward in heaven; angels do not go into a house where a dog or a picture of a creature exists. A black dog with 2 spots over his eyes is evil.

Drinking: Muhammad said do not eat and drink while standing. If one does, he must vomit. Drunk's punishment is beating.

Eating: Eat with the right hand, Muslim should lick their fingers after they eat or have some one else lick them.

Eclipse: Muhammad thought it is a sign from Allah; it might be a sign to mark the last day or the end of the world.

Eve: Because of Eve, women are unfaithful.

Evil Eye: Gabriel prayed to protect Muhammad from an evil eye.

Famine: Mohammad prayed to bring famine upon his enemies.

Farting: Farting during prayer interrupts angels talking to Allah; Angels stop asking forgiveness for you.

Fasting: Fasting during the month of *Ramadan* is an obligation for all Muslims for heavenly rewards. Fasting can be in behalf of a dead person or in behalf a sick person.

Five Pillars: Faith, Fasting, Jihad, Hajj, and Zakat.

Force: Allah commanded Muhammad to use force to spread Islam.

Forgiveness: All past sins are forgiven for a Muslim who sincerely prays during the month of fasting, *Ramadan*, or on the night of *Qadar*. Before prayer, *ablution* is for washing past sins for forgiveness. Good deeds cancel bad deeds. If a Muslim says "*Amen*" at the same time the angels say it, all his past sins are forgiven. Go on *Hajj*, do good and your sins are forgiven. Performing *Umera* is expiation for all previously committed sins. A Muslim who dies in *Jihad*, all his sins are forgiven. If at the time of death, a person who says "*No God except Allah and Muhammad is the Prophet of Allah*", all his sins are forgiven. A Muslim should not confess his sins in public. No forgiveness for a Muslim who murders other Muslims, only Hell for him. Repeat a prayer 100 times and all your sins are forgiven.

Funerals: Muslims should stand during all funeral processions. If you join a funeral procession, you will be rewarded in heaven. If you stay till the burial, you get a greater reward. Only men are allowed to carry the coffin.

Gabriel: Angel Gabriel has 600 wings, only Muhammad saw Gabriel who revealed the Quran to him. Gabriel operated on Muhammad, opened his chest and cleansed his heart before his flight to heavens. Muhammad said that Gabriel is the Holy Spirit.

Gambling: Gambling is a sin and forbidden in Islam.

Garlic: Muhammad would not eat garlic because he did not want to offend Gabriel by bad breath. He commanded his followers not to eat garlic before they go to the mosque; angels are offended by the garlic smell.

Gold: Muhammad wore a gold ring then changed his mind and forbid men to wear gold. He commanded not to eat or drink in gold or silverware.

Good Deeds: Best deed is to believe in Allah and his messenger.

Graves: Muhammad could hear the dead suffering torment in their graves. Sitting on and praying toward graves are forbidden.

Greeting: Muhammad commanded Muslims not to greet the Jews or Christians first.

Hadith: Saying of the Prophet recorded after his death. *Sahih Al-Bukahri* is the most reliable source of *Hadith* records. Muslims consider the Prophet's sayings indispensable in understanding the Quran.

Hair: Muhammad said that a Muslim man should cut his hair and trim his mustache. He cursed women who wear false hair (wig).

Hajj: Muhammad commanded that Muslims must visit the Holy *Kaabah* at least once in lifetime. Through performing *Hajj* and certain rituals, sins are forgiven.

Healing: Muhammad mixed his spit with dust and prayed for healing.

Incantation can be used for healing.

Heat: A hot day's heat is from Hell.

Heaven: Die in *Jihad* to go to heaven. If a Muslim receives booty or war spoils, his heavenly reward is cut short. People are predestined for heaven or hell.

Hell: Muslims who fight and kill other Muslims go to Hell. Women are a majority in hell. Hell is a lake of fire with a bridge that every one will pass over it. A Muslim who does not pay *zakat*, a compulsory charity, will go to hell. Those who commit suicide go to hell. People who go to hell are imprisoned there forever, but Allah may allow them out for saying" *no one has the right to be worshiped but Allah and Muhammad is the Messenger of Allah.*" Picture painters, photographers and image- makers would suffer the most in hell. People are predestined for heaven or hell. Hell has different levels of punishments.

Hijab: The woman's face cover or scarf. Muhammad's wives were ordered to fully cover themselves. A Muslim female ought to wear hijab.

Holy Spirit: Muhammad claimed that Angel Gabriel is the Holy Spirit.

Houris: Angelical beautiful virgins who inhabit the Paradise. Die in Jihad and you will enjoy sex with 72 *Houris* forever.

Illiterate: Muhammad is called to be the apostle to the illiterates. Although Muslim scholars say Muhammad himself was illiterate, a *Hadith* provides evidence that he could read and write.

Imam: The *Imam* is the most knowledgeable believer, privileged by Allah to lead his fellow Muslims in prayers.

Inheritance: Males inherit more than females.

Injustice: Muhammad had freed a Muslim who murdered a Jew. Muhammad said, "Even though the Jew should not be killed, he would go to hell any way."

Interest: Muhammad curses a person who accepts or pays interest, the person who record it, and the two witnesses who observe the transaction.

Islam: An Arabic word meaning to surrender. A Muslim must confess that there is no God except Allah and that Muhammad is the Messenger of Allah.

Jesus: The Quran revealed that Jesus is the spirit and the word of Allah. He was born without sin; He spoke in the cradle, healed the sick and raised the dead. Jesus will come again as a ruler, break the cross, kill pigs and stop the *Jizya;* a tax imposed on the Jews and Christians.

Fight against *Goog-Magoog* and force people to convert to Islam. Deity of Jesus as the Son of God is condemned. People saying Jesus is the Son of God irritate Allah. Muhammad denies Jesus crucifixion and resurrection.

Jews: Muhammad cursed the Jews and said that Allah punishes them in their graves. He said that the Jews go to hell. Muhammad declared war against the Jewish tribes of *Banu Qainuqa, Khaibar, Banu Quraiza and Nadir.* Muhammad wanted the Muslims to exterminate the Jews.

Jihad: Jihad is an Arabic word means to struggle fighting the enemies of Islam. Muhammad ordered his followers to Jihad against the Pagans of *Mecca*, to attack and rob the trade caravans in route to Mecca. He ordered Muslims to fight against those who disbelieve in Allah. Muhammad said that Paradise is gained only through *Jihad*. If a man is killed in *Jihad*, all of his sins will be forgiven and he will be awarded in paradise. Muhammad said, "*The gates of Paradise are under the shadow of the swords*".

Jinns: Spiritual creatures are made of fire. Muhammad claimed that he wrestled with a Jinni who wanted to tie him up and said that he recited the *Quran* to overpower him. The defeated *Jinn* became a Muslim. *Jinns* steal things at night and burn houses.

Jizya: Jizya is a tax imposed on the non-Muslims (Jews and Christians) who live under the Islamic rule. The tax rate depends on how prosperous they were. *Jizya* will be abolished upon Jesus second coming.

Judgment: Muhammad said he does not know what would happen to people in their last judgment, he said even himself is subject to judgment and asked for Allah's mercy. Muhammad said that Allah reveals your destination to you before you die. Allah judges men's hearts for their intentions. There will be an interpreter between man and Allah. Alcoholics will not get a drink in the after life.

Kaabah: The Kaabah in Mecca existed before Muhammad's time, the Pagans did the pilgrimage to Kaabah same as Muslims do to this day. The Kaabah was burned and demolished totally in a civil war; Muhammad then re-built the Kaabah, he placed a rare black stone that believed was handed from Adam to Abraham. The Kaabah is the most holy place on earth for Muslims.

Khadija: The first wife of Muhammad, she was 15 years older than him. She was from a Christian family and his only wife until her death in 620 A.D.

Lilat-Al-Qadar: The night in which the Quran is revealed to Muhammad. Prayers in *Lilat-Al-Qadar* are answered and sins are forgiven.

Last Day: The last day is the Day of Judgment. *Hadith* records many signs of the last day; Muslims fight each other, few people will be alive at that time, shepherds will build big buildings, fire from *Hijaz*, famine, turmoil, war, people want death, murder, no self control, and the *Kaabah* is destroyed.

Left Hand: Muslims should not eat with the left hand because Satan eats, drinks, gives, and receives with left hand.

Liquor: Forbidden even as a medicine.

Lizard: Lizards may have been humans cursed by Allah, so Muhammad would not eat it.

Lying: Muhammad justified lying and breaking oaths for the right reasons. It is okay to tell a lie for 3 reasons: when in a battle, for conciliation between friends, and between a man and his wife.

Marriage: Allah allowed Muhammad to take 14 wives at the same time, but allowed his followers only 4 wives at one time.

Miracles: Muhammad implied that he did no miracles. *Hadith* tells a story that Muhammad has split the moon into 2 parts.

Muhammad: the Prophet of Islam proclaimed that he is the last messenger of Allah. He claimed that *Gabriel* revealed to him the *Quran*, and took him in a *Night Journey* to meet Allah and see both paradise and hell, in his way back he visited Jerusalem. Muslims consider Muhammad as the most perfect man, and the best example of a true Muslim. Muhammad said that he is afraid of the torment of the grave and prayed for deliverance from hell. Muhammad justified lying; he broke his promise, cursed people, ordered looting and killing of Jews. The Hadith described Muhammad as light skinned, good looking, semi curly hair, big hands and feet and medium build. Muhammad said he does not know if he would end up into heaven or hell.

Monkeys: Muhammad asked Allah to curse the Jews and convert them into pigs and monkeys.

Moon: It is said that Muhammad had split the moon with his finger into two parts.

Murder: Muhammad ordered death and murder to those who criticized him. Muhammad forbids Muslims to kill each other.

Music: Musical instruments are Satan's tools and are forbidden in the Quran.

Muslims: Muslims are called followers of Muhammad, Muhammad said that all people are born Muslims, but an infant's faith is changed by their parents. Muslims must be united and should not fight each other.

Noah: Contradicting the Bible story, Ahadith says that Noah's son drowned in the flood.

Nursing: Nursing babies (breastfeeding) from the same female makes them brothers and sisters and they become not permitted to marry each other. This saying of the prophet Muhammad is taken as grounds for divorce of two married couple if found to be breast-fed by the same woman.

Oaths: Muhammad broke an oath; He said do not swear by your fathers, swear by Allah.

Obedience: Muslims swear to obey Muhammad, same as they do obey Allah. Muslims must be obedient to their parents and to the *Imam*.

Oppression: Muslims should not oppress on other Muslims.

Orphan: If you take care of orphans you will gain rewards in heaven.

Pagans: Muhammad ordered his followers to massacre the pagans. Bridge across hell is taken from Pagan sources. Pagans inhabited pre-Islamic *Mecca*. Pagans fast same as the Muslims do. Pagans ran the hills of *Safa* and *Marwa* same as the Muslims do. Pagans circled the *Kaabah* same as the Muslims do. Muhammad ordered his followers to follow many of the pagan practices.

Paradise: A place in heaven prepared for the believers who die for sake of *Allah* in *Jihad*, Muhammad said 'Paradise *under the shadows of swords*". Muhammad claimed that he was ascended in a *Night Journey* to heavens and visited Paradise.

Pebbles: Muslims in *Hajj* throw stones at *Satan* during the ritual of *Safa* and *Marwa*

People: All people are born Muslims, but their parents change their faith to other religions.

People of the Book: In the *Quran*, Muhammad called the Jews and the Christians, people of the Book. They know the word of God.

Persecution: When Muhammad started preaching his Message in *Mecca*, the leaders of *Quraysh* persecuted him.

Pictures: Muhammad cursed picture makers and said that angels do not go into a house having pictures or paintings. Image making or painting is an act of sin and is forbidden, but pictures can be printed on garments.

Pigs: Muhammad cursed the Jews, and Allah changed them into Pigs and Monkeys.

Poison: a Jewish Woman poisoned Muhammad. Muhammad said that incantation could be used as healing from a snake or scorpion. Dates from certain region near Medina contain an antidote from poison and magic.

Poop: Muhammad ordered Muslims not to face *Mecca* when pooping, and not to use the right hand to clean oneself after pooping.

Porn: Sex with a child is allowed. Muhammad married *Ayisha* when she was a child, only nine years old.

Prayer: Do *ablution* before praying; concentrate when you pray and your previous sins are forgiven. The *Imam* is to be followed during public prayer. The rituals for prayer is to stand, face down, raise hands, and do not pass in front of some one praying. People who do not come to community prayers in the mosque will go to hell. Prayer may be delayed for good reason; in a rainy day, in hot weather, or if a person is in a hurry or for a journey's sake. When you pray, face *Mecca*, if you face a wrong direction, your prayer is lost. If a person walks in front of you while praying, stop him physically. Sight of a dog or a woman interrupts prayer. One prayer in the Prophet's mosque is better than 1000 prayers in other mosques. Muhammad prayed that Allah burns the homes of people who do not attend prayer at the mosque.

Predestination: A man's deeds and works are pr-destined. Heaven and Hell are already determined for people by Allah.

Property: A Muslim must defend his property to death.

Prophecy: Muhammad prophesied that in the last days, there would be more murders; less good deeds; more misery and the Muslims will fight each other.

Prophets: Muhammad said that he is the last and the crown of all Prophets; there will be no more prophets after him.

Punishment: Muslims will be tormented in the grave. Punishment for stealing is cutting the hand. Punishment for adultery is stoning the adulteress woman and lashing the man.

Questions: Muhammad could not deal with faith questions, he told Muslims not to question issues of faith.

Quraiza: a Jewish tribe that Muhammad attacked, he ordered the killing of all men, and enslaved its women and children.

Quran: Angel Gabriel revealed the *Quran* to Muhammad during a period of 12 years. Verses of the revealed words to Muhammad were collected, written and compiled after Muhammad's time. There are several versions of the book of *Quran*.

Revelation: Muhammad claimed that he received revelations through the Angel Gabriel. The *Ahadith* describe that Muhammad felt immediately before he would receive a revelation; he gets sweaty, his face becomes red, he becomes semi-conscious and snores. Muhammad received revelations from Gabriel during his battles and at times having sex with some of his wives. He said that he received a revelation from Gabriel when he was sleeping with *Ayisha*.

Revenge: Muhammad took revenge and ordered his followers to take revenge for Allah's sake.

Revolt: Muslims are required to oppose their rulers if they commit bad deeds, do not follow the straight Muslim rules and do not establish prayers.

Rulers: Obey the ruler unless he commands something sinful.

Sacrifices: Animals are sacrificed for forgiveness of sins under certain rules and rituals.

Safa and **Marwa**: A pagan pre-Islamic ritual, Muhammad ran between them and commanded the Muslims to continue the ritual.

Salvation: Muhammad said that Salvation is granted by saying "No God but Allah, offer a perfect prayer, pay *Zakat* and fast". All your sins will be forgiven even if you commit adultery or theft.

Satan: Satan is a liar comes from the East. With the exception of the Virgin Mary and Jesus, all newborn babies cry because Satan touches them at birth. Satan tricks Muslims to fight each other. Muslims are commanded not to eat with the left hand because Satan does. Paintings and music is works of Satan. Satan runs upon hearing the call to prayer and farts as he runs. Satan tricked Muhammad to reveal the satanic verses.

Satanic Verses: Muhammad revealed that the three pre-Islamic pagan idol Goddesses, *Al- Lat, Mennat and Al-Uzza* are the greatest after Allah. Later he regretted the revelation and said that Satan tricked him. He called the verses as Satanic.

Science: Muhammad revealed several verses that go against basic known scientific rules.

Sex: Muhammad had a sexual drive and strength of 30 men; he had sex with all of his 14 wives during the same night. If a wife refuses to have sex with her husband, the angels curse her. If a man divorces his wife three times, and desired to have her back, she must marry and have sex with another man before he can re-marry her again.

Silk: Silk is forbidden, No silk clothes are permitted for the Muslim.

Silver: Silver or gold ware is not to be used for drinking or eating. Silver rings are allowed, but gold is not.

Sin: All people are sinners, except through Allah's mercy; all humans will be destroyed on the Judgment day. Muhammad said that even he is a sinner. Allah predestined sin.

Slaves: Muhammad ordered his men to take Jewish captives for slaves. Slaves can be owned, bought and sold to Muslims. Sex with female slave as a concubine is allowed.

Spitting: Muhammad said to spit to the left side, do not spit in front or to the right.

Stars: Allah created the stars for three reasons: to decorate the sky, to guide the travelers and to use them for shooting Satan.

Stone Worshipping: Pre-Islamic Pagans inhabited *Mecca,* they were, stone idol worshippers.

Stoning: An adulteress woman is to be punished by stoning to death. Muhammad allowed a pregnant woman that confessed fornication, to give birth and to suckle, when the baby was able to eat solid food, he ordered her stoning punishment of the fornicator.

Suckling: A male who suckles a woman, becomes same as a son to her, they are forbidden to marry each other.

Suicide: Suicide is forbidden in Islam and it is a great sin with punishment into hell forever.

Sun: Muhammad said that the sun sets in water and the sun rotates around the earth.

Sunni: Is a person who follows the traditions of Muhammad.

Sunnah: It is the path following the traditions of Muhammad. If a Muslim does not follow the traditions of Sunnah, he is considered a *Kafer* (unbeliever).

Superstition: Examples: always enter with a step leading with the right foot, pray during an eclipse, horsehair brings good luck, evil eye is fact, dead people are tormented in the graves, and images of persons or creatures will come to life to torment the painter or the picture maker.

Terror: Muhammad used terror against his enemies, he ordered his followers to terrorize and destroy the unbelievers who rejected him.

Theft: Cutting the hand is the punishment for the thief.

Torah: The Old Testament of the Bible is a main source of Muhammad's revelations.

Torture: Muhammad ordered to torture people who rejected him.

Traditions: Muhammad's way of life was recorded after his death, known as the traditions of the Prophet. True Muslims follow these traditions. ***Violence***: Islam is triumphed by violence; Muhammad said that the gates of Paradise are under the shadow of swords. Muhammad wanted the Muslims to exterminate the Jews. He commanded them to declare war against the non-Muslims if they reject Islam when peacefully offered to them.

War: Muhammad declared war against all people who rejected him. ***Wealth***: When Muhammad died, his wives fought over his wealth. ***Wine***: Wine is forbidden, Muslims are not allowed to buy or sell wine.

Wives: of *the Prophet; Khadijah* was his first and only wife for 20 years, After her death, Muhammad took for himself 13 wives and an unknown number of concubines, he managed to live with them at the same time; *Sawada, Ayisha, Hafsa, Zainab, Um Salma (Hind), Juwayriya, SaJia, Umm Habiba, Asma, Shraaf, Allia, Wasna, Maria the Coptic, Maymuna,* and *Raihanah.*

Women: Women in Islam are not equal to men. Muhammad called them deficient in their mind and faith, they are ungrateful and that most people in hell are women.

Zakat: Is a mandatory charity, compulsory and enforced to be taken from the rich and given to the poor. Allah will punish those who do not pay it.

❧

"Sayings of the Prophet was recorded after his death, Sahih Al-Bukahri is the most reliable source of Ahadith. Muslims consider the Prophet's sayings indispensable in understanding the Quran, both of the Ahadith and the Quran are the basis of the Islamic Law which is the main source of legal systems applied in many Muslim countries"

❧

PART III

RADICAL ISLAM

Part III provides a review of the roots, motives and driving forces that led to the recent Islamic terrorism and divisions between radical and moderate Muslims.

Chapter 17. Jihad In Islam

Chapter 18. Radical Islam

Chapter 19. Muhammad's Cartoons

Chapter 20. Islam above Criticism

Chapter 21. Clash of Civilizations

17

JIHAD IN ISLAM

Jihad is associated with Islam's ideology and is a cause for a moderate Muslim to live in fear and to feel as being in bondage. A person becomes Muslim by birth or by converting to Islam, he just need to pronounce with conviction in presence of two Muslim witnesses, two verses known in Islam as the two testimonial verses (*Shihada*): "*There is no God except Allah; Muhammad is the prophet of Allah*"

Once a person publicly pronounces these two testimonial verses (*Shihada*), he instantaneously becomes a Muslim. If later he wanted to change his belief and denounced his Islamic faith, he returns back to be an infidel (*Kafer*). According to the Islamic law (*Shariah*) he will be considered apostate and become subject to the death penalty. To escape the death punishment, his only option is to repent and return back to recognize Islam as his own religion. Otherwise, it is the duty of every Muslim believer to carry the execution of death penalty, fulfilling the command of Allah and the Prophet Muhammad. Allah will reward the killer for obedience and good deed.

A true Muslim is he who follows the teachings of the Prophet Muhammad. Non-Muslims are those who refuse to submit and accept Islam peacefully; they must be forced into Islam. Non-Muslims must pay a special tax *(jyzia)* or be subjected to the death penalty. A Muslim believer is not allowed to voice his opinion if it is different than what is written in the Quran or if the Prophet did not say it. A true Muslim believer becomes a member of a tightly closed cult or religious community that is bound by unanimous guards of Allah, he lives in fear of loosing his own life, his freedom is just an illusion and any of his fellow Muslims has the duty to watch him closely and to judge, prosecute and eliminate him if he decided to leave Islam as his own religion.

The Quran commands mutilation and crucifixion for striving against Allah and his apostle. Muslim fanatics believe in every word that was said by the Prophet Muhammad and they use this context to justify killing of the apostates or converts rejecting Islam.

Jihad became the most ambiguous word used to fight against non-Muslims who reject Islam as their own religion, they would be given the opportunity to repent, but this chance of repentance is normally short lived, and instead of killing them, they are subjected to ostracism, denial of their oaths in court of law, and are discriminated against to hold government official offices and positions of employment.

Prophet Muhammad said that a Muslim who dies struggling in sake of Allah, he will be rewarded in paradise and will be granted every wish he may desired during his life on earth. He will enjoy unlimited sensual pleasures offered in paradise of richness, palaces, pastures, rivers, fruits, virgins and much more. So many Muslims are highly motivated and have the ultimate desire to die in Jihad for a guaranteed admission into paradise escaping the punishment that is set for sinners who will be cast into the everlasting hell fire.

Prophet Muhammad said that only those who are martyred in the name of Allah would be saved from his wrath and anger. The prophet could not offer other way to escape the everlasting suffering, except the mere mercy of Allah. Muhammad said to his followers "*All people are and remain sinners, they shall be judged and punished by Allah in the last day, they shall suffer in the lake of fire burning forever"*. His followers asked, what about you, O' prophet of Allah? He answered: *"even me I will be punished, except if Allah provides mercy upon me"*.

Although most of the September 11, 2001 (911) attackers and the London bombers were highly educated people and are graduates of universities, the ideology of Islam made them suicides. Moderate Muslims say that Islam has been hijacked by fundamentalists similar to *Osama Bin Ladin*, the chief of *Al Qaida* who twisted terrorism as Jihad in the name of Allah. The indivisible unity between the state and religion institutions is implanted in the core of the ideology of Islam; it is the main drive of the continuing Islamic holy warfare. This kind of violence was the case with the Western Christians until the 17th century when the enlightenment led them to separate the state and the church institutions, thereby eliminating the reasons of religious warfare and allowing civilization and economic expansion to follow.

The world community fight against fractions of Radical Muslim extremists and terrorists brings to mind the moral story displayed in the classical Disney animated movie, the *Lion King*, a story of a happy and peaceful animal kingdom ruled by a righteous Lion King, his hateful brother *Scar* plotted to kill him through a deceitful plan, arranged for what appeared to be accidental death, and let *Simba*, the young cub son and heir of the Lion King to runaway fearing for his life, *Scar* took control as the King after entering in an evil pact with a wild rebel hyenas, bringing destruction, poverty and misery to all. When *Simba* grew to be the courageous adult, he returned to liberate the kingdom, concurred the evil ruler and his rebels, ended the nightmare and restored peace to the kingdom.

This classic moral story is exactly what extreme Taliban and other radical Muslim fractions similar to *Al- Qaida, Huzb-Allah* and the *Muslims Brother Hood*, who are classified by the United Nations as terrorist organizations operating in Afghanistan, Sudan, Somalia, Egypt, Algeria, Lebanon and many other countries, their ultimate goal is "*Islam must take control and rule the World*".

Many Muslim countries adopted the extreme Islamic laws (*Shariah*) as the base and main source of Islamic judicial system of the land. Unfortunately they promote Jihad, violence, killing, oppression, punishment, and discrimination creating pain to all people, both Muslims and non-Muslims. Some of these countries have recently realized and discovered the dangers of these extreme Islamic laws, so they acted to reform and are recently motivated to change their laws.

⁊

"An extreme Muslim is a believer compelled to kill any person who resist or reject Islam, he may martyr himself in jihad for the sake of Allah and the prophet Mohammad, believing that this is the only path to paradise!

Escaping the everlasting hellfire in the hereafter."

⁊

18

RADICAL ISLAM

On November 4-6, 2006, Fox News broadcasted a documentary film entitled *"Obsession, Radical Islam's war against the West"*; millions of viewers around the world watched the movie. The movie portrays Islamic extremists calling for arms against the West. This is the first of its kind that reveals insider's views of the hatred that radical Muslims have against the

West, their incitement of Global Jihad and their goal of world domination.

The documentary included reviews of several expert commentators having first hand accounts of the Islamic radical movements, among them is a former Muslim terrorist of the Palestinian Liberation Organization (PLO), a daughter of a Palestinian martyred Muslim guerilla leader, and a former Nazi's youth commander. The commentators clearly concluded that the threat of radical Islam is real and the world should be concerned, the Muslim religion is being hijacked by a dangerous foe, which has no respect of human life, seek to destroy the shared values that we stand for, and challenges the core of life and civilization. It is clear that the Islamic culture is moving to a head collision with the rest of the world.

After the horrific 911 attacks, many Americans ask: "*Why do they hate us? What have we done wrong? Why do they go so far to hurt us?*" One of the interviewed experts said "*we need to better understand Islam*" pointing to the Muslim world with its complex cultural, economical, political and extreme religious ideology that produce the suicide bombers and drive the moderate

Muslims to become fanatics, the fanatics to become extremists, the extremists to become radicals and the radicals become terrorists

All other commentators agreed that the propaganda and the teachings of the Islamic scholars and the general education to the Muslims main stream, promoting hatred, naming America as the Satan of the world, the Jews as the enemies of Allah, the Christians as infidels, those who dispute the Holy Quran must die and they call death to America. Their goal is to convert the whole world into Islam. The movie documented an extreme Egyptian clergy who lives in London, preaching his fellow Muslims in a Mosque in London, saying, "Non-Muslims are like cattle; you can take them to the market place to be sold or slaughtered". A young British born Muslim man who recruits British Muslim youth to join an Islamic terrorist organization, said in an interview: "*if it is necessary, I would kill British solders if they stand against Islamic goals.*"

One of the commentators said,

"*We must be wrong about those who came to America and instead of becoming a part of American way of life, they wanted to enforce their own agenda, to impose their way of live, and to enforce Islam to be the law of the land, we must realize that Jihad had came to America.*"

911 World Trade Center Attack Photo

Another commentator said *"Nineteen Arab Muslim fundamentalists, were welcomed to come to America, they went to U.S. flight schools, trained to fly U.S. commercial planes, hijacked U.S. planes and flew them into U.S. buildings to kill U.S. citizens."*

A former Nazi youth commander said,

"If we cannot learn from the events of the Nazi Germany, we will not be able to grasp the real danger that lies in the hatred ideology of Islam

demonizing the non-Muslims, the Christians and the Jews. Muslim's terrorist culture is parallel to the then Germany Nazi's culture where the young children and youth were robbed of their childhood and youth are taught to hate the other and carry dangerous missions for what so called noble cause. Some of us cannot connect the dots together to see the similarity between the two fascist pictures."

The fanatic Muslim terror attacks as known to the world had come into prominence after the World War II. The Islamic Brotherhood, an Egyptian strict Islamic movement was established just after World War

and grew fast after the 1948 war between the Arabs and Israel. After the 1967 war between Egypt and Israel, many radical Islamic movements have pursed their battle on variety of fronts. Examples are sectarian violence against Coptic Christians in **Egypt**, hijacking airplanes, subway bombings in **Paris**, attacks in **Russia** and many other countries around the World. The common dominator between the Muslim terrorists lies in the Holy book of *Quran* and the Prophet Muhammad's *Ahadith* (sayings and traditions).

Following are abstracts for some known and well-documented Islamic terrorist attacks, they provide an over whelming evidence in court of humanity against those who argue and defend Islam as being a religion of peace. They indicate the depth, scale and trend of these serious violent acts that took place. They are not just limited to attacks on the U.S. and western Embassies; killing U.S. Ambassador to Afghanistan, and taking Americans hostages or burning churches in countries ruled by Islamic laws:

Muslim assassinated President Anwar Sadat of Egypt in 1979.

- Attacking American Marines in **Beirut**; bombing of restaurants in **Spain**; Hijacking of TWA flight 847 bound from **Athens** to **Rome** and taking Americans and other passengers hostages until they release 766 Lebanese prisoners being held in **Israel**.

- Exploding a car bomb outside a USO club in **Naples**, **Italy**.

- Exploding Pan Am Boeing 747 flight 103 from **London** to **New York**.

- Fire bombing bookstores in **Berkley**, **California**, the store was selling Salman Rushdie's book "*Satanic Verses*".

- In **Egypt**, attacking the Monastery of Saint Mary's in the village of El-Muharrak and killing a monk.

- Blasting the Israeli Embassy in **Buenos Aires**, **Argentina**.

- Radicals attack Christians in villages of El-Quosya, **Egypt**, destroying their homes, businesses and killing seven.

- Shooting and killing two CIA employees and wounding others near the gate of the CIA head quarters, **Langley**, **VA** by a Pakistani Muslim who lived in the U.S.

- Bombing of the parking garage below the **World Trade Center, New York**.

- Ambush against U.N. peacekeeping forces in **Somalia**, bombing a building housing Jewish Organizations, killing at least 85 and injuring more than 200.

- In **Buenos Aires**, exploding Philippine Airlines Flight 434 killing a Japanese businessman.

- Hijacking Air France flight to **Algeria**.

- Attacking U.S. consulate vehicle in **Karachi**, **Pakistan**, killing two

- U.S. diplomats.

- Car bombing U.S. Military headquarters in **Riyadh**, **Saudi Arabia**.

- Suicide bomber attack on the Egyptian Embassy in **Islamabad**, **Pakistan**; Radical Muslims attack Coptic village of El-Badary, **Egypt**, destroying their homes and killing seven.

Khobar high rise buildings were housing U.S.
Allied forces personnel, Saudi Arabia.

- In **Saudi Arabia** a fuel truck bomb explodes outside the Khobar high-rise buildings housing U.S. and allied forces enforcing the no fly zone over southern Iraq, 19 U.S. air force personnel are killed and more than 500 others wounded.

- In **Algeria**, a bomb exploded the home of the French Archbishop, killing him and his chauffeur after a meeting with the French Foreign Minister.

- In **Paris**, a bomb exploded abroad a subway train, killing four and injuring 86.

- In **Egypt** 12 Coptic Christians are murdered in the village of Abu Qurcas.

- In *New York* a Palestinian Muslim opens fire on tourists at an observation deck atop the Empire State Building, killing one and wounding many, then he killed himself.

- In *Jerusalem*, two suicide bombers exploded themselves in a market place killing 14 and injuring 150.

- In *Karachi, Pakistan*, four Americans were killed as they drove from the Sheraton Hotel.

In Egypt, 58 Western tourists were killed and 28 others wounded at the Hatshepsute Temple in the Valley of Kings near Luxor.

*In **Nairobi, Kenya**, twin car bombs blasts the U.S. Embassies*
killing at least 247 and wounding more than 500.

- In *Jerusalem*, a suicide car bomb explodes in main food market killing two and injuring 25 others.

- In *Coimbalore, India*, a series of bomb blasts killed 43 and injured 200.

- In *Islamabad*, six rockets were fired at the U.S. information Cultural Center and the United Nations offices.

- In **Egypt;** a raid by Muslim fanatics on the Coptic Christians while they were praying in a church in the village of El-khosheh, killing 11 Christians.

- In *Yemen*, suicide bombers abroad a small boat attacked the U.S. destroyer USS Cole at the port of Aden, 17 U.S. sailors were killed and more than 30 injured.

- In *Israel*, a Hamas suicide bomber exploded himself in a popular Tel-Aviv nightclub killing 21 and injuring more than 120.

- In *New York*, the 911 hijacked planes, American Airlines flight 11, and United Airlines 175 crashed in the *World Trade Center towers*, another hijacked American Airline flight 77 crashed in the *Pentagon*, a fourth hijacked plane, United Airlines flight 93 crashed in a field near *Shanks Ville, Pa*. Approximately 3000 people were killed in the simultaneous attacks.

- In *Indonesia*, terrorists attacked a church; killing three people;

- In *Pakistan*, gunmen opened fire on a church in a town of

- *Bahawalpur*, killing 18 and injuring nine people.

- In *Nigeria*, Armed Muslims attacked Christian village community killing five.

- In *Pakistan*, a wall street Journal reporter, Daniel Pearl, was kidnapped and killed by Islamic militants.

- In *Egypt*, a Coptic Church was attacked by armed radicals who set fire into it, destroyed several of their cars and homes, 10 people were injured.

- In *Jordan*, a car owned by a Jordanian anti-terrorism unit was detonated by a timing device, killing an Egyptian and Iraqi worker were nearby a food shop.

- In *Pakistan*, a grenade attack on a church killed five including an American woman and her daughter, 45 others were injured.

- In *Israel*, a suicide bomber blew himself in the Park Hotel in *Netanya* where 250 people had gathered in a banquet hall celebrating the Passover Seder (ritual meal), 29 were killed and 130 injured.

- In *Tunisia*, a suicide bomber crashed and detonated a propane gas truck into a historic Synagogue, killing 16 persons including 11 Germans, one French and 3 Tunisians and injuring 26 others.

- In *Indonesia*, Muslims attacked a Christian village killing 12 and injuring 6; In *Karachi, Pakistan*, a vehicle parked next to a Navy Shuttle bus exploded, killing 10 French Nationals, 2 Pakistanis and wounding 19 others.

- A car bomb exploded near the U.S. consulate and Marriott Hotel in *Karachi, Pakistan*, 11 people were killed and 51 wounded including one U.S. and one Japanese citizen.

- *In Pakistan*, terrorists attacked a Christian Missionary School in town of Jhika Gali, six were killed and four injured.

- In *Philippines*, six missionaries were kidnapped, two were subsequently beheaded.

- In *Kabul, Afghanistan*, a blast occurred at midday outside a store selling televisions and satellite dishes, which are forbidden under Taliban.

- In *Al-Dhabbaah, Yemen*, a small boat carrying a large amount of explosives rammed in a French tanker, killing one person and wounding four others.

- In *Kuwait*, a gunman attacked U.S. solders while they were conducting a non-live-fire exercise, killing one U.S. Marine and wounding one other.

- In *Bali*, a car bomb exploded in a busy tourist area filled with nightclubs, cafes and bars, killing at least 187 tourists and injuring about 300 others.

- In *Russia*, 50 armed Chechen rebels took control of a culture theater, during a 3-day siege, in a rescue attempt, the Russian special forces stormed the theater, killed the rebels and 124 hostages died.

- In *Indian Kashmir*, Islamic Militants raided a Hindu Temple Complex, 11 were killed and 50 injured.

- In *Mombasa, Kenya*, three suicide bombers drove a vehicle into the front of the Paradise Hotel and exploded, killing 15 people and wounding 40 others. In *Mombassa, Kenya*, two Anti-craft missiles were launched but missed downing Boeing 757 taking off to Israel.

- In *Makassar, Indonesia*, a bomb exploded in a McDonald's restaurant, killing three and injuring 11 others.

- In *Daska, Pakistan*, a grenade attack on a church killed three and injured 14 others.

- In *Philippines*, Islamic liberation Front, attacks a mini bus, killing nine and wounding four.

- In *Riyadh, Saudi Arabia*, suicide bombers attack three gated residential compounds for foreign workers and setoff car bombs, killing 35 and wounding over 200.

- In *Casablanca, Morocco*, five simultaneous bomb attacks occurred at restaurant, hotel, Jewish cemetery, Jewish community center and the Belgian consulate, killing 33 and injuring 101.

- In *Kabul, Afghanistan*, a taxi rigged with explosives rammed into a bus carrying a group of German peace keepers and international Security Assistance Force (ISAF) heading to the air port for their return home, five were killed and 29 wounded.

- In the village of **Kfar Yavetz, Israel**, Islamic Jihad claimed responsibility for a suicide bombing which killed a woman an injured three others.

- In **Katra, India**, a bomb exploded near a Hindu Temple, killing six and caused extensive damage to the temple.

- In **Jakarta, Indonesia**, a car bomb exploded outside the Marriott hotel during rush hour, killing 10 and wounding 150, the explosion caused extensive damage to the hotel building.

- In **Baghdad, Iraq**, a bomb truck drove into the driveway of Canal Hotel housing the headquarters of the United Nations, and exploded, killing 23 and wounding100 others.

- In **Baghdad, Iraq**, a suicide bomber detonated a car packed with explosives outside the Baghdad Hotel Housing the Iraqi Government leaders of U.S. contractors, at least 8 people were killed and as many as 40 wounded.

- In **Riyadh, Saudi Arabia**, a suicide car bombing killed at least 17 people were killed and more than 120 killed.

- In **Kanawha, Afghanistan**, a car bomb exploded outside the United Nations Assistance Mission in Afghanistan (UNAMA), killing one person, and injuring other and causing major damage to the building.

- In **Istanbul, Turkey**, a car bomb exploded at the Beth Israel Synagogue, killing four and wounding 60.

- In **Istanbul, Turkey**, a bomb exploded at the Never Shalom Synagogue, killing 16 and wounding 240.

- In **Istanbul, Turkey**, a bomb detonated outside the HSBC bank, killing 11 people and wounding 105 others.

- In *Yelwa, Nigeria*, at least 78 Christians were killed and several churches destroyed by armed Muslims.

- In *Mariveles, Philippines*, a radical Muslim group of Abu Sayaff claimed responsibility of an explosion on a ferry that killed nearly two hundred people.

- In *Madrid, Spain*, a series of coordinated terrorist bombing against commuter train system, killed 191 and wounded more than 1800 people, making them the deadliest terrorist attack against civilians in Europe since Lockerbie bombing in 1988.

Photo, Madrid commuters train bombing.

- In **Kano, Nigeria**, Muslim mob attacked Christians, 11 were burned to death and two churches were set on fire.

- In **Sylhet, Bangladesh**, at least two people were killed by a bomb blast at a shrine, some 50 others, including a British diplomat were injured; In **Ambon, Indonesia**, a blast in a Christian sector of the city kills one and injures 13, another bomb found near a church and was defused.

- In **Pattani, Thailand**, Muslim radicals kidnapped a Buddhist civilian and de-captivated him; they left a note attached to the body, warning other Buddhists of the same fate.

- In **Khobar, Saudi Arabia**, a shooting rampage and hostage standoff in the Saudi's Oil industry hub killed 22 and injured 25, mostly foreigners.

- In **Riyadh, Saudi Arabia**, the BBC's security correspondent Frank Gardner was critically injured and his cameraman Simon Cumbers was killed when they came under fire.

- In **Riyadh, Saudi Arabia**, Robert Jacob, an American working for Vinnell Corporation, a U.S. defense contactor working in Riyadh, was gunned down.

- In **Saudi Arabia**, U.S. hostage Paul Marshal Johnson, an American engineer working for Lockheed Martin, was kidnapped and beheaded.

- In **South Kashmir**, Muslim terrorists abducted and slit the throats of a railway engineer, Sudhir Komar Pundeer, and his brother.

- In **Jakarta, Indonesia**, Muslim fanatics raided on a church service in Eastern Indonesia, killing the priest and wounding four people, the attack occurred near the town of Poso, the site of a bloody Muslim-Christian clashes that killed some 2000 people since 1999.

- In **Moscow, Russia**, near a busy subway station a suicide bombing killed 10 and injured 21, the incident took place exactly a week after two Russian Airlines crashed within minutes of each other killing 90 people, Islamic group calling itself " Islambouli Brigades" claimed responsibility; In Russia, a group of Islamic rebels stormed a school and took 1200 children and adults captive, a siege ended after 3 days with the deaths of at least 339 hostages, about half of them children, 500 others were injured.

- In **London, England**, Suicide bombers struck central London's public sub-way during morning rush hour, 52 were dead and 700 injured.

London's public two level bus bombing.

- In **South Hall, England**, a Muslim man stabbed his sister to death in front of his two young daughters in so called honor killing, In Islam a Muslim woman is not allowed to marry non-Muslim man.

- In **Sharm El-Sheikh, Egypt**, three bombs exploded in the tourist resort town, 83 were reported dead and 200 injured.

- In **Bangladesh**, simultaneous bombing in almost every province carried out by radical Muslims, two dead and more than 100 injured from the attacks.

- In **Lubumbashi Mines in Congo**, a shipment of smuggled uranium 238 uncovered by customs officials in Tanzania, was transported from Lubumbashi mines in Congo and destined for the Iranian port of Bandar Abbas, in nuclear reactor, Uranium 238 can be used to breed Plutonium used in nuclear weapons.

- In **Sydney** And **Melbourne, Australia**, the Australia Security Intelligence Organization (ASIO) discovered one of the largest homegrown extremists Organizations whose members are trained overseas.

- In **Amman, Jordan**, a nail bomb detonated outside a market place in a predominantly Christian area, 8 were dead and 45 injured.

- In **Maiduguri, Nigeria**, thousands of Muslims attacked Christians, burned at least 15 churches and killed at least 16 during demonstrations against the cartoons of the Prophet Muhammad, since the year 2000, several thousands of people died in violence fueled by adoption of strict Islamic Shariah law.

- In **Ontario, Canada**, Canadian police and intelligence officials made arrests of 17 Canadian Muslims who were charged of planning terrorist attacks on targets in southern Ontario, the groups accepted delivery of three tons of Ammonium Nitrate, a common fertilizer that can be used in making explosives.

- In **Slagelse, Denmark**, Danish police made arrests of nine Muslims after the murder of 18 years old Ghazla Khan, she married against her family's wishes, more than 50 reports of honor killing related crimes are filed in Denmark, it is against the Islamic law for a woman to marry a non-Muslim man.

- In *Miami, USA* seven Muslim men were arrested in an alleged plot against the Sears Tower, and a Federal building in Miami, they said that their target was to establish and build an Islamic army to kill as much of the devils as they can.

- In *Bombi, India*, a series of blasts rocketed commuter train at rush hour, 200 were dead and 700 injured from the attacks.

- In *Tabah, Israel*, a car bomb exploded in front of a hotel in a busy resort during the Jewish religious holy day of Yum Kapur.

- In *Pakistan*, a fanatic Muslim exploded himself after shooting Prime Banazir Bhutto, a leader of Democratic party in Pakistan, she was assassinated and may others were killed on December 26, 2007.

This long list of terrorist and criminal acts is growing every day; it represents the evidence of the nature of violence, bloodshed and the dark side of Islam.

Lack of understanding and ignorance of the Americans and Westerners of what real Islam is about; have literally invited the horrific sequels to the disasters that have already perpetrated against us. A majority of the western people does not even know what the Arabic word "*Jihad*" means; they had no worries until the Muslim terrorists (*Jihadists*) came to us through our gates. Their goal remains to force the whole world into Islam, and for them to rule the whole world.

It is interesting to note that this goal of ruling the world remained the same since the early times of Islam, and that the same aggressive rebel groups and obedient warriors continued to this day. Calls for arms and jihad seem to be answered by indoctrinated energetic young men to provide them devotion, earn respect of their community; make their leaders and families proud of them. They also became motivated by the promise of glory, luxuries and virgins in the next life. They are surrounded and trapped by the same hatred and blood lust ideology that their ancestral parents of early Islam had embraced. It is a huge human tragedy and travesty spanning for generations with little hope of redemption. The radical Muslims of today have the same drives and goals of their Arabian ancestors who spread Islam by the sword.

Terror in Islam is rooted deeply by its divine commands of Allah and the Prophet Muhammad. It is entrenched in the preaching, commands, injunctions, inspirations, practices and examples set by the Prophet Muhammad and by his contemporary followers, who lived by the sword and used it as the most potent weapon to subdue adversaries who happened to cross their path.

Mohammad Al Ghazoli, a Muslim Scholar who came to Christ, author of the book: "*Christ, Muhammad and I*" he wrote:

"It is clear that Islam rose on the foundation of terrorism, where it began by raiding, stealing and robbing the caravans of Quraysh that traveled between Damascus and Mecca, ending with the assaults on the Jews wherever they are in Khaibar or Medina, and later against the Christians of Medina and Taif (in the Arab peninsula). The Muslims, throughout their history, followed the steps of the founder of the Islamic religion"

❧

"An extreme Muslim believer is he who follows the teachings of true Islam as revealed, in the book of Quran and said by the Prophet Muhammad, most likely he cannot be other than a terrorist."

❧

19

MUHAMMAD'S CARTOONS

In February 2006 when the *Tyllands-Posten,* a Danish newspaper published caricature figures of the Prophet Muhammad, millions of Muslims around the world up roared defending the prophet's untouchable character. Muslims believe that Prophet Muhammad is the most righteous and most holy person that Allah chosen from all men to be the last messenger to the world.

Critics describe the cartoons as Islam-O-Phobia and argue that they are blasphemous. On the other hand, supporters of the cartoons claim that they illustrate freedom of expression and right of opinion to the same degree their Muslim extremists and terrorists exercise their right of free speech. Cartoons about other religions are frequently published and followers of Islam are not singled and targeted in discriminatory way.

The Danish newspaper Tyllands-Posten stated: "*in our opinion, the twelve drawings were sober, they were not intended to be offensive, nor were at variance with the Danish law, but they have indisputably offended many Muslims for which we apologize.*"

One of the cartoonist explained "*The general impression among Muslims is that the cartoons are about Islam in a whole, it is not. It is about fundamentalist aspects, which of course are not shared by the majority of Muslims.*"

According to the BBC, Muslim scholars claim, "*It is the satirical intent of the cartoonists is to associate the prophet with terrorism that is so offensive to vast majority of Muslims.*"

Why the insult is so deeply felt by some Muslims? Of course, there is the prohibition on images of Muhammad, but one cartoon, of the *Prophet wearing a turban shaped as a bomb with a burning fuse*, implies a depiction of Islam. It extends the caricature to Muslims in general and to Muhammad himself as a terrorist. This will certainly display a widespread perception in the West and to people across the world that Muslims harbor hostility, sponsor violence to achieve their goals and make people fear Islam and Muslims.

Other cartoons clearly mock Muhammad regarding his revelations of what Allah had promised and prepared for the Muslim martyrs if died fighting for His sake. For example, a cartoon shows the Prophet lifting up his hands to stop the souls of suicide bombers saying, "*The paradise is running short of virgins.*" Another cartoon shows an angel escorting a soul of a dead Muslim to the gatekeeper of paradise announcing, "*He claims that he just died in the cartoon riots defending the Prophet Muhammad, asking if he qualifies for admission into paradise and if he will have 72 virgins?*"

The Islamic law (*Shariha*) and the traditions of Islam consider insulting the Prophet as one of the most serious crimes. Such a violation warrants death. Modern Muslims in Western Europe and the United States, say that the problem is deeply rooted and associated with extreme versions of Islam, but not with Islam and Muslims as a whole.

Some say that the publications of the cartoons and the predictable riots that took place are part of coordinated effort to smear the image of Muslims and Islam, influence public opinion in the western countries and to support the military intervention against what is called terrorism in the Middle East. Other Muslim leaders say that the cartoons were published to influence and widen the split between the Muslim Arabs in the Middle East and the Christian West to justify their support to Israel.

Muslim masses across the Arab world raged violently protesting the insulting cartoons, burning churches, attacking embassies, desecrating flags and calling death to the enemies of Islam.

In Palestine, armed men stormed the offices of the European Union in Gaza demanding an apology from Denmark and Norway.

Saudi Arabia recalled its ambassador from Denmark, *Libya* followed like wise, *and Syria* issued strong worded statement denouncing the offence against both the Arab and Islamic communities and calling upon the Danish Government to take the necessary steps to punish the culprits and see that such offences are not to be repeated in the future.

In Jordan the Danish Ambassador was summoned by the Jordanian Minister of Foreign Affairs to express Jordan's protest.

In Egypt, the Egyptian Parliament called upon the government to withdraw its ambassadors to Denmark and Norway.

In Lebanon, Hezbullah (Party of Allah, an extreme Islamic organization) described the cartoons as a grave offence to Islam.

In Kuwait, religious scholars called upon the members of the Kuwaiti Parliament to see how to put an end to such offence against the feelings of Muslims. Hundreds of Kuwaitis demonstrated in front of the Danish Councilors demanding an apology to all Muslims.

The Arab Foreign Ministers denounced the Danish Government for its refusal to take any action against the Tyllands-Posten newspaper, expressing their disappointment with the European Human Rights Organizations that in their view have failed to take a firm Pro-Islamic position in this case.

In Iraq, Muslim rioters attacked and burned Christian Churches. *In Yemen* protestors demanded boycotting both Danish and Norwegian products until such time they apologize.

In the United Arab Emirates, the Minster of Justice and Islamic Affairs, criticized the cartoons depicting the Prophet as an immoderation and excess of all acceptable intellectual norms, saying in no way it could be regarded as freedom of expression as stated by the Danish authorities.

In Iran, Lebanon and Syria the Danish embassies have been set ablaze to fire, several Middle Eastern countries have recalled their ambassadors from Denmark. The Iranian government said it is reviewing the trade ties with countries where the cartoons were published. Denmark issued a list of 14

Muslim countries that Danish travelers should avoid and urged its citizens to leave the country of Indonesia.

Almost everywhere in the *Arab Emirates* and *Saudi Arabia* businesses have withdrawn Danish products from shelves in their stores and from major outlets. They displayed notices stating, "*We do not sell Danish products*". People all over the Arab world encouraged each other to boycott the Danish goods.

Muslim leaders, Mullahs, and people of different origins appeared on the Islamic television net works supporting the outrage and spoke that freedom of speech does not mean insulting the other, and that one should not cross over a red line of respecting other beliefs.

The U.S. State Department Spokesperson Sean McCormack said *"We understood why many Muslims found the cartoons offensive, we found on Friday, the cartoons offensive. But we also spoke out very clearly in support of freedom of the press. As to what is broadcast over the air waves, those are decisions in free countries for free media."*

The Western reactions were obviously different, questioning where the Mullahs and those good Muslims were when the beheadings of Western hostages took place. Where they were when the up roaring extreme Muslim crowds attacked and burned churches? When the World Trade Center was attacked? When *Jill Carroll or Margaret Hassan*, the woman who overtly expressed solidarity with the Iraq's people; an executive director of CARE in Iraq providing help and support to the needy Muslims; still was assassinated? Where are the ordinary good Muslims in the Islamic world, why they were not pouring and raging into the streets to demonstrate against Saudi Arabia's Semitic policy that prevent the Jews and Christians from stepping on the soil of Mecca, merely because they are Jews and Christians?

Of course there are many Mullahs, Imams and Muslims who are sincere and are in favor of peace; of course they exist, but a real conflict also exists because the incompetence, inequality of ideological, social and historical issues. No Muslim has the courage to change or alter the traditional ways, which the Prophet of Islam has established for the Muslims setting their relationships with the non-Muslims. Many believe that Muhammad's sacred revelations and sayings had set conflict and division in the World.

Supporters of freedom of speech, compare the Muslims response for earlier controversies with the recent controversy of the cartoons.

An example is the novel book of *Satanic Verses*, by *Salman Rushdie* was published in 1988 and inspired in part by the life of Muhammad. The title refers to the satanic verses revealed in the Quran for the deity to three pre- Islamic idols goddesses beside Allah. Upon publication in 1988, the novel caused much controversy, as many Muslims considered it contained blasphemous references. *Ayatollah Ruhollah Khomeini*, who was the supreme leader of the Islamic Republic of Iran, issued an order to all the Muslim believers (*Fatwa*), calling for the death of Rushdie. He said that it is the duty of every Muslim to obey and carry out the order. However in the U.K., the book was acclaimed and it was a 1988 Book Prize Finalist, eventually losing to Peter Carey's "*Oscar and Lucinda*". On February 14,1989, the Ayatollah broadcasted the following message on the Iranian radio, "*I inform the proud Muslim people all over the world that the author of Satanic Verses book; which is against Islam, the Prophet and the Quran; all those involved in its publication and are aware of its content to be sentenced to death.*"

As a result, *Rushdie* went into hiding. *Hitoshi Igarashi*, the Japanese translator of the book was stabbed in July 1991, *Ettore Capriolo*, the Italian translator, was seriously injured by stabbing in the same month, and *William Nygaard*, the publisher in Norway, survived an attempted assassination in Oslo in October 1991. On February 14, 2006 the Iranian state owned news agency reported that the Khomeini's *Fatwa* would remain in effect permanently.

The Muslim people's violent riots all over the world, boycotts of Danish products, demands that the United Nations to adopt resolution to protect religious icons, that the Danish government to apologize, punish the offenders and to withdraw the cartoon publications. Reports without borders concluded that the reaction in the Arab World "betrays a lack of understanding" of freedom as an essential accomplishment of democracy.

Many Western News Media commentators said that nowadays, we live in a world where political, religious and other views on variety of subjects are mocked and reticulated. Comparing to the modern Western liberal mentality, the Muslim World is not flexible, but impulsive and oversensitive. We are facing a situation where Muslims feel transgressed against, yet it can be also said that they are over reacting. The intent of the cartoonists is to make a political point and the only difference between a cartoon and an essay, is that a cartoon makes a point with drawings rather than words.

Others say that the cartoons are just an excuse for really angry Muslims to express views of their tyrannical governments, their poverty, and their diminished stature in this technological world that they fear and has left them far behind.

The Sunni Muslim scholars insist that depicting the prophet Muhammad is prohibited so people do not fall into idolatry and revering the messenger instead of his message. In response, some explain, "*No one believes that Muslims are at risk of worshiping images of Muhammad depicted in the cartoons, or those images that were created hundreds of years ago that were created by Muslims and presently are displayed in Fine Art Museums. It takes a retarded person or a child to think that paintings that depict Muhammad could lead people to worshiping him.*"

Certainly, there is no shortage of books in the libraries or movies that are showing in the theaters all over the world, or the routine Muslim programming in Arabic television stations that did not mock Christianity or Judaism. Some ask how those Muslims who have trouble respecting other faiths; assume the creditability and integrity to demand from the world to hold freedom of expression and to respect their beliefs?

The Islamic laws (*Shariah*) are rules taken from Islamic doctrine and Ahadith; some are designed to crush moderate Islamic and other religions doctrines. Accordingly, no one is allowed to challenge a rule that applies a verse in the Quran or a Hadith (saying) of the prophet. The violent verses of the Quran cannot be renounced and the secular science cannot be permitted. Clearly these strict laws chill and stifle freedom of religion, thought, and speech. One may ask, can or will Muslim scholars revise or remove past classical violence that rooted in the Quran and Ahadith (sayings) of the prophet? If Islam really holds the ultimate truth and final revelation, then it should not fear any challenge.

Many paintings of Muhammad created by Muslims themselves are now in museums and on the World Wide Web; some are published here in this book. Production of photos and motion pictures fall under the category of pictures that is horrible sin in Islam. However, it is always said that Allah will punish those people on the Day of Judgment, but there is no command for Muslims to go out now and punish those painters or picture makers. In the most authoritative sources of Islam, there is no particular emphasis on forbidding pictures of prophets or the person of Muhammad in particular. It is clear that Muslims should not make pictures of Muhammad only as an application of general prohibition against making pictures of people or animals.

Western leaders and commentators say that logic must be challenged with logic, and a reason should not be silenced by the sword. Violence of corporate punishment, boycotting of products of a country or withdrawal of ambassadors and burning of flags, are violent acts to suppress freedom of expression that has no place in the free western society.

When a religion suppresses free speech and dissent, it testifies against itself. What the religious leaders are trying to hide? Why they want criticism shut down? The leaders should be able to defend it by words only, for its appeals should be self-evident.

Can Islam reform itself ? Can moderate Muslims persuade the more traditional strict Muslims who adopt the Shariah Islamic laws, teachings and sayings of Muhammad, especially those regarding Jihad and fighting the unbelievers? This is hard to imagine because it would open the door for many unconvinced Muslims to leave the burdensome and severe Islam.

"In the most authoritative sources of Islam, there are no particular emphasis forbidding pictures of prophets or the person of Muhammad in particular. It is not clear that Muslims should not make pictures of Muhammad, but only is ruled as a general prohibition against making pictures of people or animals."

20

ISLAM ABOVE CRITICISM

Muslims are hypersensitive to any criticism or observation that does not glorify or honor their religion and specially their Prophet "*Muhammad*". Islam tolerates no such dissent or discussion of any kind. In

Islamic countries, the punishment for insulting the prophet is death.

On September 12, 2006, *Pope Benedict XVI* at the University of *Regensburg* in Germany said a lecture entitled "*Faith, Reason and University- Memories and Reflections*". Many Islamic politicians and religious leaders protested against what they said, it is an insulting mischaracterization of Islam contained in a quotation by the Pope of the following passage.

"*Show me just what Muhammad brought that was new and there you will find things only evil and inhuman, such as his command to spread by sword the faith he preached*".

The passage originally was written in 1391 A.D., as an expression of views of the Byzantine emperor *Manuel II Paleologus* on such issues as forced conversion, holy war and the relationship between faith and reason. *Pope Benedict XVI* commented: *"Violence is incompatible with the nature of God and the nature of the soul."* After saying that, Muslims up roared and raged all over the world:

In *Egypt,* the Vatican envoy was summoned and a statement by the foreign Minster referred that the Pope's statement shows that there is a lack of understanding of real Islam.

In *Palestine* attacks with firebombs on Orthodox and Angelical churches in the West Bank city of Naples.

In *Somalia*, Sheik *Abubukar Hassan Mlin* of Somalia's supreme Islamic Court Council urged Muslims "Wherever you are, hunt down the Pope for his barbaric statements as you have pursued *Salman Rushdie* the enemy of Allah who offended our religion. Whoever offends our prophet should be killed on the spot by the nearest Muslim".

In *Kuwait*, a high-ranking official called on *Pope Benedict XVI* to apologize for his remarks, and called on for all Arab and Islamic states to recall their ambassadors from the Vatican and to expel those from Vatican until the Pope apologize for the wrong done to the Prophet of Islam.

The Islamic Guardian Council of Iran declared that the speech of the Pope was a part of "a series of Western conspiracy against Islam," saying that he (the Pope) had linked Islam to violence and challenged Jihad while in the same time he apparently closed his eyes to crimes being perpetrated against defenseless Muslims by leaders of power and hypocrisy under the flags of Christianity and Jewish religions.

One of the most influential Muslim clerics asked that the Pope must fall on his knees in front of senior Muslim cleric, apologize and try to understand Islam. Numerous statements of disappointment and demands for an apology have been issued in response to the Pope's remarks. Officials of **Yemen, Morocco, Turkey, India, Indonesia and Malaysia** issued threats of severe diplomatic actions.

On the other hand, statements from officials in the United States, Australia, and Europe had a different view of the Pope's speech as being an invitation for dialogue between religions and rejects any type of violence.

Muslim religious leaders, groups and organizations all over the world demanded that *Pope Benedict XVI* to apologize for his remarks about Jihad and Muhammad; they called it "Character assassination of the Prophet Muhammad."

Pope Benedict XVI.

The Vatican's chief spokesman announced in a statement that the Pope had not intended to carry out an in-depth study of Jihad, nor the Muslim thinking about it, even less to offend the sensitivity of the Muslim faithful. Careful reading of the Pope's lecture would show that what really matters to the Pope is a clear rejection of religious motives for violence.

On September 17th Pope Benedict XVI issued a statement that he did not intended to offend the Muslims, he expressed his deep sorrow for the reaction of Muslims in some countries for a few passages in his speech, saying it was a sincere and frank invitation to a dialogue with great mutual respect.

On September 25th, Pope Benedict XVI held an audience with Muslim diplomats, ambassadors of Muslim countries and representatives of appointed consultative body of the Islamic affairs. In the meeting, the Pope reiterated his conviction that the dialogue between Muslims and Christians is "a vital necessity". It is for the good of a world marked by relativism, one that "excludes the transcendence and universality of reason. At this meeting Pope Benedict XVI expressed all the esteem and profound respect that he has for Muslim believers.

People in the free world who read the text of the lecture say that the Pope simply quoted an early medieval text, did not say he agreed with it, the lecture was not really about Islam at all, and yet the whole Islamic world went into uproar. They also say that they could not see any offence to Islam, Muslims are the ones who are so touchy that they cannot allow anyone speak his mind or express his opinion, not even to quote a mildly critical sentence from 700 years ago. The point of violence in Islam is purely historical fact and any researcher has to be blind to ignore the connection between Islam and violence. Recently many Muslim Scholars try to explain and clarify that Islam is a religion of peace; they virtually reflect nothing of what is written in the Quran and Ahadith about jihad.

It is not surprising that the West struggles to understand people that their faith cannot take even the mildest critique without burning flags, attacking churches and chanting death threats. The Danish cartoons could genuinely be seen as an offensive to Muhammad, but this lecture has no offense what so ever, except for those who are determined and do not allow any dialogue or criticism.

The Pope's lecture was in part a call for all religious communities to conduct themselves in a nonviolent, non-coercive and rational manner. Anyone who carefully reads his lecture can clearly see that this debate has been blown way out of proportion. The question that remains is what is wrong with Muslims? This kind of out of control, overreaction and violent response will only alienate the West from Islam even more, and confirm the stereotyping and distrust between both sides.

❧

"If Islam really holds the ultimate truth and final revelation, then it should fear no challenge, the leaders should be able to defend it willingly and without threat of violence. On the other hand, if people want to leave it, then they should be allowed without persecution or a sword hanging over their heads."

❧

21

CLASH OF CIVILIZATIONS

Muslim apologetics explain that the recent violence around the world is a result of a clash of religions and civilizations between Islam and Christianity, Arabs and Westerns.

Peaceful and successful integration of Muslims into Western societies is now more critical than ever before. In England, France, Denmark, Netherlands, Spain and the United States, millions of Muslim immigrants became citizens of their new homeland of choice, however, they continue struggling to integrate themselves into their new society. Their struggle is stemmed from whom they should give allegiance to? A Muslim believer must give allegiance to Allah and His messenger Muhammad, not to a state or any other authority, particularly not to a Christian or to an Infidel led community. Islam's teachings do not recognize a state that is run by a secular government, but rather to an *Umma*, or nation ruled by Islamic Laws and led by clergy leaders of *Imams* and *Mullahs*.

Lately, many western countries came under the test to face a growing role of Muslims who live in their societies. The newly formed Muslim communities are suspected as a threat to their law of land and way of life. It became clear that integrating Islam in these countries depends upon whether a Muslim, in his new home country, can abide with its laws, differentiate between freedom of belief and allegiance to the state, encourage peaceful integration and discourage extremism.

The controversial 2004 event in France of banning headscarves (*hijab*) in public schools and governmental institutions is an example that clearly demonstrated how Muslims are struggling to integrate themselves in their new home countries. Riots, violence and serious threats by Muslims trying to enforce Islamic culture and ideological standards in France had been rejected.

In an interview aired on the Arabic Al-Gazira TV on February 21, 2006, addressed the issue of clash of civilizations in a debate between a Muslim Scholar, and an Arab American Psychiatrist; *Waffa Sultan* explained: The clash we are witnessing around the world is not a clash of religions, or a clash of civilizations, it is a clash between a mentality that belongs to the Middle ages and other mentality that belongs to the 21st century.

It is a clash between civilization and backwardness, between the civilized and the primitive, between barbarity and rationality. It is a clash between freedom and oppression, between democracy and dictatorship. It is a clash between human rights on one hand, and the violation of them on the other hand. It is a clash between those who treat women like beasts, and those who treat women like human beings.

What we see today is not a clash of civilizations; civilizations do not clash, but compete? The Muslims are the ones who began using this expression; the Muslims are the ones who began the Clash of Civilizations. The Prophet of Islam said to his followers "*I was ordered to fight the people until they believe in Allah and his Messenger.*" When Muslims classify people into Muslims and Infidels, and call for the Muslims to fight the non- Muslims until they submit and believe, they are the ones who started the clash, and began this fight. In order to stop this war, they must re-examine their Islamic books and curricula, calling and naming a non-believer "*kafir*" and urging Muslims to fight the infidels.

Waffa Sultan commenced saying: what civilization on the face of this earth that allows a Muslim scholar to call people by names that they did not choose for themselves? Once he calls them *Ahl-Al-Dimmah* (an Arabic term that refers to non Muslims who live under the rule of the Islamic Law), then he calls them the *people of the book* (a term that refers to the Jews and

Christians), yet another time he compares them to *Apes and Pigs,* or he calls the Christians those who incur Allah's wrath. Waffa Sultan exclaims why they are called the *people of the book*? They are people of many books; all the useful scientific books that Muslims use today are the fruit of their free and creative thinking. What gives a Muslim scholar the right to call them "*those who incur Allah's wrath or those who have gone astray*" and then he says that Islam commands to refrain from offending the beliefs of others? Continued to explain, she said, "I am not a Christian, a Muslim or a Jew, but I am a Secular human being. I do not believe in supernatural, but I respect other's right to believe in It." this angered, the Muslim Scholar, so he impulsively called her a heretic and blasphemer against Islam and its Messenger. The Psychiatrist replied saying "You may believe in stones, as long as you don't throw them at me, you are free to worship whoever you want, but other people's beliefs are not of your concern, whether they believe that the Messiah Son of Mary is God, or that Satan is God, let people have their beliefs."

The Jews have come from the tragedy of Holocaust and they forced the world to respect them by their knowledge not by their terror, by their work not by crying and yelling. Humanity owes most of the discoveries and science of the 19th and 20thcenturies to Jewish scientists. Fifteen million people, scattered throughout the world, won their rights through work and knowledge. We have not seen a single Jew blow himself up in a German restaurant; we have not seen a single Jew destroy a church; we have not seen a single Jew protest by killing people. The Muslim Taliban has turned three ancient *Buddha'* Statues into rubble, we have not seen a single Buddhist burning down a mosque, killing a Muslim, or burning down an embassy. Only Muslims defend their beliefs by burning down churches, killing people, and destroying embassies. This violent path will not yield any results; Muslims must ask themselves what they can do for others, before they demand that others respect them.

Muslim scholars around the world have expressed that the terrorist criminals similar to Osama-Bin-Laden have violated the teachings of traditional Islam led to committing the horrific acts against the United

States. The self professed true Muslim, Saudi exile, the chief terrorist, leader of *Al-Qaeda* and a prime suspect in the September 11, 2001 attacks, he is number one on the FBI most wanted list.

Answers to the famous questions, what went wrong? And why do they hate us? Point out to the terrorist radical Muslim minds, the process of their making and how they are matured. That's where parents, teachers, neighbors, clergy, community leaders and governmental authorities can play a role and are responsible of the outcome.

No one had yet found acceptable logical answers to these famous questions, but discovered lack of critical imagination and arrogance of the tribal mentality have perpetuated the ancient assumption that use of the sword is the only way to deal with people who disagree with spread of Islam. When a person identifies himself strictly with a religion rather than being a human, he does not realize that a part of his identity is religious that belongs to God, and the other part is human belongs to people. If the human part is overshadowed by a radical religious ideology, then that person could lose control of his own human logic, he could become religiously fanatic and may give up his own life for his beliefs.

Terrorism has different facets, different levels of severity and different circumstantial causes. Its roots start growing with mistrust and end up bringing people and communities in disrepute. Terrorists segregate themselves from others, by planting negative ideas in their minds. They became indifferent and destined to be unable to connect with the others and actually end up hating their successes, the first step in the direction of inhumanity and terror. The war on terror is therefore mostly a clash of cultures, worldviews, ideas, narrative history, or chosen glories.

We may continue to increase budgets for counter terrorism efforts, build more walls, prison cells, security gates, increase military forces and more homeland security. We may continue to form longer lines in airports, wait for our turn to take off our shoes and be searched for a safe flight. This may be necessary, but we should not forget the real roots of the problem and should think how to provide solutions and avoid being a part of the problem. The more walls we build around ourselves today, the more we have to tear down when we finally realize that we actually need each other.

We should continue to contribute more to help Muslims to develop their humanity with better education, spreading awareness to change their lack of sense of belongingness, to expand their vision and help them to learn to be tolerant towards other people, religions, cultures, colors and ethnic origins. At an early age a child need to learn how to love and not to hate, how to accept other people and recognize those who are different and not the same. Lately, more advanced modern countries and International Organizations including the United Nations became aware that the world need to increase humanitarian assistance to those troubled regions. Globalization is working fast through interaction of trade, travel, and advancements of the Internet and satellite television media. The once large earth has become a small village, now we instantly feel the joy and the suffering of other people around the globe. Indeed our shared humanity is based on the idea that security and well being of any one community, one nation or one people is connected and interdependent on the well being of others.

Mutual respect, understanding and co-operation among Muslims and different religions could be achieved if they stop using force to change the other and if they understand that a person becomes evil if his actions tear down the human soul and rob it of dignity and joy.

Governments of some Muslim countries similar to *Egypt, Jordan* and *Arab Emirates* are very concerned and they try very hard to reform their societies toward democracy, observance of human rights, and promoting equality for all people irrespective of gender, religion, origin, or race. There is now much powerful plea to create stable and peaceful relations between Islam and other people.

"It is a clash between freedom and oppression, between democracy and dictatorship. It is a clash between human rights on one hand, and the violation of them on the other hand. It is a clash between those who treat women like beasts, and those who treat women like human beings. What we see today is not a clash of civilizations; civilizations do not clash, but compete." **Waffa Sultan**, *an Arab American Psychiatrist*

PART IV

THE WAY TO SALVATION

art IV explains why a Muslim's only hope is the Mercy of Allah on the Day of Judgment and why Jesus Christ is our hope for salvation.

22

WRATH OF ALLAH

The word "salvation" cannot be found in the dictionary of the Quran; but what can be found is many promises of reward to those who do good and warnings of punishment to those who do evil. For those who believe in Allah and the Prophet Muhammad, the reward will be paradise, while punishment and suffering in the everlasting Hell will be the reward for unbelievers.

"Those who have disbelieved and died in disbelief, all of the earth's gold would not be accepted from any of them if offered as ransom. They will have a painful punishment, and they will have no helper" (Quran 3:91).

No one will be allowed a second chance after death, *"When they are set before the fire (Hell) and they say: would we return* (to earth again for a second chance)*, we would not reject the verses of Allah but we would be of the believers"* (Quran, 6:27)

Prophet Muhammad said much about Hell and Wrath of Allah: *"The happiest man in this world will be among those to be doomed to the fire (Hell), on the Day of Judgment he will be dipped in the fire once, then he will be asked: "son of Adam, did you ever see any good? He cries O' Lord have mercy!"*

On the other hand, the one who turns away from the Quran will have a life of hardship in this world. *"But whoever turns away from the Quran, he will have a hard life, and we will raise him up blind on the Day of Judgment"*

(Quran, 20:124)

Prophet Muhammad said to his followers that Allah forgives only those who convert to Islam. When someone converts to Islam, Allah forgives all of his previous sins and his evil deeds. After converting to Islam, the person will be rewarded for his good or evil works according to the following saying of the Prophet: *" Your Lord who is blessed and exalted is most merciful. If someone intends to do a good deed but does not do it, a good deed will be recorded for him. And if he does do this good deed, he will be rewarded ten to seven hundred or many more times, and will be recorded for him. And if someone intends to do a bad deed but does not do it, a good deed will be recorded for him, but if he does do this bad deed, a bad deed will be recorded against him"* (Hadith pre Sahih Muslim # 131).

Although Muslims believe that humans are predestined, they believe that they have free will, and that they are responsible for their choices for which they are accountable.

On Day of Judgment (Day of Resurrection), all people will be resurrected; each will be judged according to his beliefs and deeds. Every person will stand in front of Allah and the angels will read out his record of good deeds and bad deeds. If his good deeds overweigh his bad deeds, he will be admitted into paradise, but if his bad deeds overweigh his good deeds, his judgment will be pronounced to send him to the everlasting pit of :fre (Hell). No salvation, no second chance, unless if Allah granted him mercy. Allah is so forgiving and most merciful.

Muhammad said that on the Day of Judgment, those who died Muslims while believing will be saved *"Those who die while believing there is no true God but Allah, and Muhammad is the messenger (prophet) of Allah", will be admitted to paradise forever, but those who die while disbelieving and are not Muslims will be losers and will be sent to Hell Fire; "And whoever seeks a religion other than Islam, it will not be accepted from him and he will be one of the losers in the Hereafter"* (Quran 3:85).

Muslims believe in Divine predestination (Al-Qadar), *"Whatever God's will to be will be"*, because of the following reasons:

- God is the creator of every thing.

- God knows everything. He knows what has happened and what will happen.

- God has recorded all that has happened and all that will happen.

- What God wills to happen does happen and whatever He wills not to happen does not happen.

- Muhammad described the life in the Hereafter as a very real life. It is not only spiritual, but physical as well. People will live there with their own souls and bodies. Life of the present world when compared to the Hereafter is like a few drops of water compared to the vast water of the sea.

- A person is saved when he says with conviction in Arabic; *"La Ilaha illa Allah, Muhammad rasul Allah,"* which means, *"There is no God except Allah and Muhammad is the Messenger of Allah."* saying these two testimonial sentences converts him to Islam and he becomes a Muslim, he should also do the following:

- Believe that the Quran is the word of Allah revealed to his messenger Muhammad.

- Believe in the Day of Judgment (the day of Resurrection), is true and will come, as Allah promised in the Quran.

- To accept Islam as his or her only religion.

- Not to worship anything or anyone except Allah.

- In the Quran, Muhammad repeatedly said that there is nothing but the mere will and mercy of Allah that keeps sinners at any one moment out of hell.

- The Quran affirmed what previously came in the Torah and the new testament of the Bible concerning the righteousness of God dealing with the sinners that is observed through:

- God has no desire to cast sinners into hell, but they must be judged according to His divine justice. It is not easy for us to imagine how fearful for sinners to stand before God at whose rebuke the earth trembles, and before whom the mountains fall down.

- Sinners deserve to be cast into hell, so that God's divine justice never stands against God's using his power to punish the sinners who did not repent before standing before him.

- Sinners are under a sentence of condemnation to hell; they justly deserve hell to satisfy the sentence of the law. The eternal and immutable rule of God's righteousness has been :fxed between Him and mankind, gone out against them and stands between them and God; so every unsaved man belongs to hell where justice and sentence of God's unchangeable law takes place.

- All sinners are subject to the very same anger and wrath of God that is expressed in the torment of hell. Hell is prepared and the :fre is made ready to receive them, the flames do rage and glow and the pit have opened its mouth under them.

- Satan is waiting and stands ready to fall upon and seize the sinners as his own; they belong to him. God allowed him to have their souls in his possession, and keep them under his dominion. The Bible represents them as his good: "The devil watches them; He is ever by them at their right hand; he stands waiting for them like a greedy hungry beast.

- Sin is the ruin and misery of the soul; it is destructive in its nature and if left without restraint, there would be nothing else to make the soul perfectly miserable. The corruption of the heart of man is immoderate and boundless in its furry; and while wicked men live here; without God's Spirit, they are exposed to sin which is like :fre of hell that is restrained by the will of God, so if sin was not restrained by man, it would turn the soul into :fery hell of :fre.

- There is no known way for men to predict the moment when they will die. There is no assurance for a man to predict the moment that he may depart out of this world. Sudden death may be by accident or invisible danger, unseen and unthinkable; God has so many innumerable and inconceivable means of taking the wicked men out of the world and allow Satan to grip them for eternal punishment in hell. Man's own liability because not being prepared for early and unexpected death is unlimited and priceless.

- All sinners hope to escape hell while they continue to reject God's word and salvation, and so they remain wicked and unsaved from hell. Almost every person who hears of hell, flatters himself that he shall escape it; he depends upon himself for his own salvation; he flatters himself about what he done, what he is now doing, or what he intends to do. Every one lays out matters in his own mind, how he shall avoid damnation, flatters himself that he contrives well for himself, and that his schemes will not fail. He knows there are but few that will be saved, and that greater number of people who died is gone to hell. He imagines that he lays out matters better for his own escape than others have done. He does not intend to come to that place of torment; he says within himself, that he intends to take effectual care, and to order matters so for himself as not to fail.

- In the Quran, as well as in the Old Testament of the Bible, God did not promise to keep man out of hell, or to give him eternal life, nor promised any deliverance or preservation from eternal death, but what the Old Testament of The Bible described is the covenant of Grace, "a promise that God will send a Messiah, in whom all the promises of forgiveness of sins, peace between man and God and salvation of man can be achieved". The birth, cruci:fxion and resurrection of Jesus Christ have ful:flled God's promise of the Covenant of Grace. Surely, this promise is not for those who have no interest in this promise, who do not believe in any of the promises of conciliation between God and man, and those who have no interest in our Lord and Savior Jesus Christ, the Mediator of the Covenant. Muhammad clearly denied the salvation of Jesus Christ. Muhammad told his followers to trust in him and to follow his example to avoid punishment in the Last Day of Judgment.

Muhammad taught his followers that the most superior way of asking for forgiveness is to pray, *"O Allah, you are my Lord, no one has the right to be worshiped except you. You created me and I am your slave, I am faithful to **your covenant and your promise,** I seek your refuge with you from all evil I done. I so entreat you to forgive my sins, for no one can* *forgive sins except you"*. Although Muhammad denied Jesus' salvation, he here refers to what is written in the Old Testament of the Bible (Torah) that God offered for all humanity and was ful:flled by the birth, cruci:fxion and resurrection of Jesus Christ almost six centuries before his time. Muhammad died uncertain of his destination saying that all humans shall go to Hell.

So, if you do not accept Jesus Christ as God's promise of the covenant of Grace as your savior, you will loose your chance of salvation, and cannot escape God's justice and enforcement of his eternal law. You have done nothing to at least appease or abate God's judgment, you are to be sentenced to the pit of hell, and suffer the executions of the :ferceness of his wrath. God is not bound by any promise to save you or delay your judgment for one moment. The devil owns you and is waiting for you; hell is gaping for you, and the flames of hell gather, flash and ready to swallow you up. There are no means within reach that can be of any salvation to you. In short, you have no refuge; nothing to take hold of; all that you could hope for is the grace and mercy of un-covenanted and un-obligated God. All your righteousness would have no more influence to uphold and keep you out of hell, other than acceptance of Jesus Christ as your Lord and Savior.

If you wish to experience a change of heart by the mighty power of the spirit of God, if you wish to be born again for eternal life, and if you want to rise from being dead in your sins, if you did not experience the light and life being in the hands of a loving God, the following love thought is for you:

"My mother did not raise me to be a slob, on the contrary she taught me that my cleanliness is next to godliness, dirt, spots, smudges were a kin to calamity, it was hard for me to make it through a day without spilled food during a meal, stained from mud in a rainy day, or an ink spot from a leaky pen, my mother taught me that there is only one chance to make good impression, she would not be amused by me hiding because of my grubbily appearance, she taught me that admitting a wrong doing is the :frst step to recovery. My mother was willing out of her own love to always wash my clothes and keep me clean.

Similarly, God taught us how to keep out of sin, abide with His word and follow His commandments. God would not be amused that you come back to him sloppy, grumpy, troubled, and spotted all over with sin. God loves you; He is waiting for you to admit and confess your sins, He wanted you to repent than to perish. He offered to you out of his own love, Jesus Christ, to show you the way for forgiveness and for cleansing of your sins. Would you take this opportunity and accept God's free offer of Salvation.

ↆ

"Muhammad in his prayer refered to God's covenant and promise, The Old Testament of The Bible described the Covenant of Grace, a promise that God will send a Messiah, in whom all promises of forgiveness of sins, peace between man and God and Salvation of Man can be achieved"

ↆ

23

JESUS IN THE QURAN

Prophet Muhammad said that both the Quran and the Gospel are the word of God and both are written through the spirit of God, however the two books contradict each other. Muslim theologians like *Al-Tabari* (died A.D. 855), *Al-Bukahri* (died A.D. 870), and *Al-Gazzali* (died A.D. 1111) believed in the authenticity of the (Greek) Gospel text, and that it promotes same message as the Quran: *"Say ye, we believe in Allah, and the revelation given to us, and to Abraham, Ishmael, Isaac, Jacob and the tribes and that given to Moses, and Jesus, and that given to all prophets from their Lord, we make no difference between one and another of them."* (Quran 2:136).

"I (Allah) was who revealed the law (to Moses), there was guidance and light, if any do fail to judge by the light of what Allah hath revealed, they are unbelievers. We sent Jesus, the son of Mary, confirming the law that had come before him, we sent him the Gospel; Therein was guidance and light, a guidance and an admonition to those who fear Allah. Let the people of the Gospel judge by what Allah hath revealed; they are those who

rebel. Judge what Allah has revealed, and follow not their vain desires". (Quran 5:47-52)

Muhammad speaking to the Christians and the Jews, said it is God's order to believe in his word that was revealed (before his time) in the Torah and the Bible: *"Say we believe in the revelation which has come down on us and which came down to you".* (Quran 29:46). Later, Muhammad said that the Christians had corrupted and changed the Word of God that was revealed in the Gospel.

It is quite clear that at the time when the first copy of the Quran was written, around 650 A.D., there was no evidence of possible corruption or unreliability of the Bible. If the Bible were corrupted before or at the time of Muhammad, the Quran would not affirm that the Bible is the Word of God. The thousands of manuscripts of the Bible that are pre-dated Muhammad's time by hundreds of years give proof that the Bible could not be corrupted. The idea that the Bible is corrupted will be a conflict with the Quran's affirmation that no man can change God's word, *"No man can change the word of God".* (Quran 6:34 & 10:64).

Some Muslims say that the Quran states that the Bible was distorted: *" Ye people of the book, why do ye clothe truth with falsehood, and conceal the truth, while you have Knowledge."* (Quran 3; 71)

"There is among them a section who distorts the book with their tongues, you would think it is part of the book, but it is not part of the book". (Quran 3; 78)

These verses of the Quran were directed to people of the book who verbally distorted God's words, not with their pens but by their tongues. The twisted words did not become a part of the book, else the Quran would not command the Muslims to seek the advise of the Jews and Christians (people of the book) to understand the word of God if they do not know.

"Ask of those who posses the Message". (Quran 21:7). The integrity of the Bible has been confirmed in the Quran and by the ever increasing strong archeological discoveries and historical findings that support the authenticity of the Bible. The unanswered question, why should any one, for any reason, attempt to change the word of God, remains unanswered.

The events of crucifixion and death of Jesus Christ on the cross are explicitly and abundantly testified for in the Bible, but had been denied by Muhammad in the Quran. This is a clear conflict between what is revealed in the Quran and what came in the Bible. The Quran affirmed that the Bible is the true Word of God and that there is no man can change God's word.

The abundant testimonies of the Gospel writers, the apostles, the historical facts and the extensive arguments by many Bible critics testify to the truth of crucifixion and death of Jesus Christ on the cross.

In addition to the four gospel writers, Matthew, Mark, Luke, and John, the Bible mentions a number of eyewitness reports confirming the fact that the events of crucifixion and death of Jesus Christ had happened. Other eyewitnesses and many historians had testified to the truth of the crucifixion and resurrection events. It is known that Islam require the testimony of only two witnesses to set up the truth in a dispute. One may ask why Muslims deny the truthfulness of the Bible regarding Jesus' crucifixion and resurrection events.

Saint Peter, a Jew himself, had witnessed Jesus and later became his apostle, he preached what he have seen and touched. When he addressed a vast crowed of the Jews just seven weeks after the crucifixion, he testified:

"Men of Israel, listen to this: Jesus of Nazareth was a man accredited by God to you by miracles, wonders and signs, which God did among you through him, as you yourselves know. This man was handed over to

you by God's set purpose and fore knowledge; and you, with the help of wicked men, put him to death by nailing him to the cross. But God raised him from the dead, freeing him from the agony of death, because it was impossible to death to keep its hold on him" (Bible, Acts 2:22-24).

One of Rome's most prominent historians Cornelius Tacitus, being aggressive opponent of early Christianity wrote in the Roman Annals of wars and mighty conquer *"The name of Christian is derived from Christ, who was executed under the government of the Procurator Pilate"* (Annals 15.44).

The truth of the Bible is verified throughout the time long before the start of Islam, it is the only book with the oldest manuscripts on record. One of those old manuscripts is the Alexandrian text, it was written in the fourth century after Christ and almost two hundred fifty years before Muhammad's time, it complies totally with the text in our hands today. This manuscript is presently kept in the British museum in London.

Another old text of the Bible is the Sinai text, which was discovered in 1844 in the monastery of saint Catharine in the Sinai desert. The manuscript was written in 450 A.D. and is now kept in the British museum in London.

Two of the Bible oldest texts are kept in the Vatican, they were written in 150 and 300 A.D., the two manuscripts contain both the New and Old testaments of the Bible and are now kept in the Vatican.

The most circulated version of the Bible is the King James Version, which was translated in 150 A.D. from a Syrian text known to be the oldest manuscript ever found. Other old manuscripts of the Bible were translated before Muhammad's time to the Greek, Coptic, Aramaic, Italian, English French and many other languages.

Prophet Muhammad revealed in the Quran that Mary the mother of Jesus is the most perfect of all women in the world. The Quran confirmed the story of the Virgin Mary's annunciation and conceiving by the spirit of God to bear a holy son named Isa (the Arabic word for Jesus). While Mary was praying in the temple, an angel appeared to her announced that God chose her from all women of the world to bear a holy son. She said *"how shall it be, I did not know a man, no man touched me and I am not unchaste?" The angel said "So it is the will of thy Lord, who said that it is easy for us, and we appoint him as a sign to all men and mercy from us to all nations, it is a matter so decreed." So she conceived the child and she retired to a remote place until the baby was born.* (Quran 19:16 to 19:22)

Also the Quran reveals, *"Mary, daughter of Imran, who guarded her chaste, so that we breathed into her a life by our will, and she believed the words of her Lord and his books, and was obedient to Allah"* (Quran, 19: 6 to 19:16)

Saint Mary's Annunciation

The Quran tells us the following story; when Mary gave birth to Jesus, she carried the baby to her people, who questioned her saying "O' sister of Aaron, thy father was not a man of evil, nor thy mother a woman of unchaste". She pointed to the baby, they asked her how a baby in the cradle would talk to defend you? But Jesus spoke and said to them; " I am indeed a servant of God, he has given me revelation, made me prophet, had me blessed wherever I will be, joined on me prayer and charity as long as I live, he made me kind to my mother and not over bearing or miserable. *"So peace on me the day I was born, the day I shall die and the day that I shall be raised up to life again".* When baby Jesus the son of Mary said his statement of truth, they believed and ended their dispute.

The name Jesus is from the Hebrew word Yesu'ah, which means "the Lord Saves". God Himself gave him the name Jesus as written in the Old Testament of the Bible. The Angel of God appeared to Mary and said *"Do not be afraid, Mary, you have found favor with God. You will bear a child and give birth to a son, and you are to give him the name Jesus". (Luke 1:30-31) "He was to be called Jesus, because he will save his people from their sins"* (Matthew 1:21)

SAINT MARY THE MOTHER OF JESUS

Saint Mary the Mother of Jesus

Since the very early time of Christianity many apparitions of Saint Mary; mother of Jesus; had been recorded in the history all around the world. Here I would like to testify for what I have witnessed on April 18, 1968, 4:30 a.m. in Cairo, Egypt. Tens of thousands of people watched and witnessed an illuminating miraculous apparition of the Holy Virgin Saint Mary. The blessed mother of our Lord Jesus Christ had appeared many times on the top of Saint Mary Coptic Orthodox Church building at Al- Zeitoun, a suburb of Cairo, Egypt. It is said that this church was built on a site where the Holy family stayed during their flight into Egypt. The church is located on a very busy heavily trafficked main road named Tom-Um-Bay. Across from the church site is a large maintenance garage for public bus transportation; the facility operates around the clock every day of the week.

After the Six Days War of June 6, 1967 between Egypt and Israel; Egypt was badly defeated; shock waves went through out all the Islamic World. Muslim fanatics and radical movements all over the region called for Jihad against the Infidels, namely the Jews and the Christians. Muslim extremists were eager to persecute and even kill the infidels wherever they were found. Christians in Egypt felt the pressure of the rising wave of oppression and discrimination. Muslim extremists set fire to several church buildings; they attacked properties and robbed businesses owned by Christians. An environment of fear spread in the Egyptian streets while the Muslim government officials let confrontation to take place. On April 3, 1968, an article in a daily newspaper reported an apparition of Saint Mary had taken place at the Coptic Orthodox Church of Saint Mary in Zeitoun, Cairo.

Three Muslim maintenance workers witnessed the apparition from the garage site overlooking the church building had told the events. One worker reported that he saw an illuminated figure of a woman walking on top of the Church dome, he screamed, calling the other two workers, they rushed to see the illuminated body, they realized that it is an apparition of the Virgin Mary the Mother of Isa (Jesus), one of them rushed to report the apparition incident to a police station. In the next day, a newspaper reported the apparition story. For almost three years after that day, many apparitions were witnessed by tens of thousands of people, both Christians and Muslims. Thousands of people rushed every night with hopes to see a glimpse of the Blessed Virgin Mary's apparition.

People of every faith gathered every night waiting joyfully and patiently for an appearance. Muslims chant a verse from the Quran saying "O' Mary, God blessed and chosen you above all women of the world" and Christians were singing hymns praising the Virgin

Mary. Many people reported miracles of healing from chronic health problems or sicknesses; some of their physicians issued testimonial medical reports.

Illuminated doves some times circled around her then flew toward the East direction in organized formation and disappeared in the dark accompanied the apparitions.

Saint Mary herself a source of light, moved turning in a half circle as if she was blessing the crowd. I was stunt and deeply amazed watching the light beams scattered in every direction coming from her wavy long dress spreading over her arms down to her toes.

The apparitions ended in 1971 leaving an atmosphere of unity and peace between people. The highly charged extremists and fanatic Muslim fractions had been affected with a definite shift toward peace.

A Photo of the Apparition of Our Lady of Light the Virgin
Saint Mary at the Church of Zeitoun, Cairo, Egypt.

A view of the Saint Mary Coptic Church of Zeitoun, In Cairo, Egypt, where the Apparitions took place.

Both Governmental Authority and Holy Council of the Coptic Orthodox Church in Egypt acknowledged the apparitions of the Blessed Virgin Mary in a clear and bright luminous body. Tens of thousands of Christians and Muslims had witnessed these apparitions during numerous nights over an extended period of time from April 2, 1968 through 1971.

For more on the Saint Mary's Apparitions, log to the following Internet site: (Htt HYPERLINK "http://biblia.com/apparitions/Zeitoun.htm"p://biblia.com/apparitions/Zeitoun.htm)

MIRACLES OF JESUS

The Quran tells us that God strengthened Jesus (Isa) with His Holy Spirit and aided him by divine miracles. Jesus the infant spoke in the cradle. Jesus, the child, created a bird figure from clay, he breathed into it and let it to fly. Jesus, the man, retuned life to the dead, healed the born blind, the sick and the lepers (5:110 and 111). The Quran tells a story of another miracle that after Jesus commanded his disciples to fast for thirty days, to break their fasting, they asked Jesus to provide food for them and Jesus had descended a table full of food by the divine power of the Almighty Allah. (Quran 5:112-116). These verses are known as *"Surah of the table."*

CRUCIFIXION OF JESUS

The Quran tells us a story that Allah saved Jesus from the hands of his enemies, the Jews, and raised him up to himself. Allah had tricked the Jews who wanted to crucify Jesus, Allah replaced him with a look-alike person, Jesus was lifted up and his look-alike person was crucified in his place; The following verse of the Quran denies the crucifixion of Jesus: *"They (the Jews) say we killed Christ Jesus, the son of Mary, the apostle of God, but they killed him not, nor crucified him, but so it was made to appear to them, and those who differ therein are full of doubt, with no (certain) knowledge but only conjecture to follow, for surely they killed him not."* (Quran 4:157)

Just by this one verse, Muhammad denied the crucifixion of Jesus Christ, but all four writers of the New Testament Gospels testified to the truth of this event.

Jesus Christ crucifixion

JESUS IS ALIVE

The Quran acknowledges that Jesus was born without the seed of man, he had no human father, his mother the Virgin Mary was chosen by God. She is the only woman in the entire Quran; specifically called by name, and confirms that she conceived Jesus by God's Sprit and His Word. (Quran 3:47)

Although Muhammad denied the deity of Jesus and said that it is only the mere will of God, that Jesus was sent to the world as a prophet, the Prophet Muhammad recognized Jesus as the Messiah who is born in the flesh, not from the seed of a man but of the sprit of God, and that Jesus had raised the dead, gave sight to the blind, healed the sick, and descended a table from heaven to feed five thousand people. The Quran says that Jesus was ascended into heaven and shall come back to judge all the people in the last day. So although the Quran denied the crucifixion event, it says that Jesus was ascended into heavens providing the evidence that Jesus is alive from the very beginning until now and to the end of times, and confirms that Jesus is the judge of mankind in the Last Day. In other words the Quran confirms that Jesus is alive same as God is alive, He is the Judge same as God is the Judge of mankind.

Jesus Christ Resurrection

RESURRECTION OF JESUS

The Quran says: *"Allah raised him up unto himself, and Allah is exalted in power, wise"* (Quran 4:158).

Six centuries after death of Jesus Christ, with just a very short few verses, Muhammad claimed that Jesus is ascended alive into heavens, but denied his death and resurrection; accordingly he denied God's salvation for mankind.

Although the Quran revealed that Jesus is the Word of God, born of the Spirit of God, ascended alive into heaven and shall come back at the end of days to judge the living and the dead, Muhammad ignored the prophecies written many centuries before his time affirming the crucifixion and resurrection of Jesus Christ. He ignored all the historical facts and testimonials of those people who witnessed and spoke of the crucifixion and resurrection. Twenty years after the death and resurrection of Jesus Christ, Apostle Paul wrote his first letter to the Corinthians, testifying that the majority of some five hundred people were still alive and had witnessed the events of Jesus' crucifixion and resurrection. The prophecies in the Old Testament and the testimonies in the New Testament of the Bible affirm that Jesus;

- *Would be born from a Virgin* (Isa 7:14; Matt 1:21)

- *Would be of the seed of Abraham* (Gen 12:1-3 & 22:18; Matt1: 1)

- *Would be of the tribe of Judah* (Gen 12:1-3; Luke 3:23,33)

- *Would be of the house of David* (2 Sam 7:12; Matt 1:1)

- *Would be born in Bethlehem* (Mica 5:2; Matt 2:1)

- *Would be anointed by the Holy Spirit* (Isa 11:2; Matt 3:16-17)

- *Would perform miracles* (Isa 35:5-6; Matt 9:35)

- *Would cleans the temple* (Mal. 3:1; Matt9: 35)

- *Would be rejected by his own people, the Jews* (Psalm 18; 1 pet 2:7)

- *Would be crucified and died on the cross.* (Psalm 37: 21-22 and Isa 53:7-12; Matt 27:27-50; Mark15: 26-37; Luke 23:26-46 and, John 19:13-30)

- *Would be resurrected from the dead.* (Luke 24:46-47; John 20: 25-29; Rom10:9)

An unbiased reader can easily find that the Quran's unsupported and fanciful accounts concerning the truthfulness of the Bible has no shred of reliable historical evidence, and that the dogmatic Quran assertions concerning Jesus' crucifixion and resurrection are mistaken. The Quran affirms that no one can change what is written in the Torah and the Bible. No one can change the facts that are discovered by the archeologists and recorded by the historians. Although it is suggested that Jesus' death on the cross is viewed as a defeat, the fact is that Jesus out of his absolute strength and power had willingly scarified his life for all of us, defeated death and rose victoriously. Jesus himself spoke about this event saying *"I am the First and the Last, I am the Living One; I hold the Keys of Hades".*

One may ask why should Jesus go through all that? Why God did come to us in the flesh? The Bible tells us: *"Jesus was sent by God to be the way to the eternal life".* (John 3:16). By His death on the cross He became the ransom for all who believe in Him including those who went before. Jesus Said *"Before Abraham was born, I Am"* and said that *" Your father Abraham rejoiced to see my day, and he saw it and was glad".* (John 8:56-57) God had announced the Gospel of Christ in advance to Abraham that all nations were blessed through Jesus. (Gal 3:8-9).

Once, in a church meeting, I heard a testimonial from a Muslim lady who accepted Jesus Christ and became a very dedicated Christian. She joyfully told her story, saying: "I came from very conservative Muslim family, I often wondered and was confused why the Christians take Jesus to be their God? The Quran tells us that God Almighty is one, and those who say that Jesus is Son of God are unbelievers. One day in the midst of my deep confusion, I was very troubled, so I cried and prayed asking God to help me understand, why the Christians claim that you the Almighty One become a man? How come you who are in the highest is born in the flesh as Jesus? Why you go through all this trouble? Why you lower yourself and get born in a manger? Why you accept to live a hard life as one of us, suffer as we do, be judged, crucified by wicked people and then resurrect yourself back to heavens? Wondering about all this trouble, she continued saying, "that day, I went to the kitchen as usual to wash my dishes, I noticed a long line of small ants walking along the edge of the sink, turning downward to perish in a puddle of water. I watched them for a moment and said to myself, how can I save them? How I can warn these ants from going in the wrong direction? Muhammad said ants can speak! I wished that I could speak their language, may be I need to be transformed and become one of them, so I can warn them of going to their death. Momentarily in a flash, I saw the image of Jesus Christ in my mind, this was the very one instant moment of my life when, I accepted Him as my God and Savior".

This was the moment when I understood the incarnation and resurrection of Jesus Christ My Lord and God. Now, I understand that both the Bible and the Quran affirm the deity of Jesus, the Word of God, born through the Spirit of God, from the Virgin Mary, he has no human father, he was crucified, died, ascended into the heavens and will come again at the end of time to judge the living and the dead. The Quran clearly indicates that Jesus has the same attributes of God. In the Bible, Jesus said about himself: *"I am the First and the Last, I am the Living one; I hold the keys of Hades."* When the people asked Jesus to show them God the father, he said: *"Who has seen me has seen the father."* (John 14:9)

"The Quran says God is Alive and He is the Judge of the world. Also the Quran affirms that Jesus Christ is of the Spirit of God. He is the word of God, He is not of the seed of Man, He is Alive and He is the Judge of mankind in the Last Day"

24

GOD IS ONE

The Bible clearly speaks of God the Father, God the Son (Jesus Christ) and God the Holy Sprit, and also clearly presents that there is only One God.

The word Trinity is composed of two parts "Tri" meaning three, and "Unity" meaning One, thus: Tri + Unity = Trinity. It is a term acknowledging what the Bible reveals about God; God is three "Persons" who has the same essence of One in Trinity.

The word Trinity was not universally known until the first council of Nicene in 325 AD, the council clearly established the dogma of Trinity of One God; the Father, the Son, and the Holy Sprit; and rejected any heresies that separates the three apart.

The Bible offers many scriptures that show God is One:

- *"Hear, O Israel. The Lord our God is One"* (Deut, 6:4).

- *"I am the Lord, and there is no other; besides Me there is no God."* (Isa, 45:5)

- *"There is no God but One"* (1 Cor, 8:4).

- And after being baptized, Jesus went up from the water and behold, the heavens were opened, and he saw the Spirit of God descending as a dove, and coming upon Him, and behold, a voice out of the heavens, saying: *"This is My beloved Son in whom I am well pleased"* (Matt 3: 16-17).

- Jesus said: *"I and the Father are One"* (John 10: 30)

- Jesus said: *"He who has seen me has seen the Father"* (John 14:9).

- Jesus said: *"He who beholds me beholds the One who sent me"*. (John 12: 45).

- And the angel answered and said to her (Mary) *"The Holy Spirit will come upon you, and the power of the Most High will overshadow you; and for that reason the Holy offspring shall be called the Son of God"* (Luke 1: 35).

- The Bible tells us *"For there is one God and one Mediator between God and men, the man Christ Jesus, who gave Himself a ransom for all to be testified in due time"*. (Tim 2:5-6)

- Jesus said to his disciples: *"Go therefore and make disciples of the nations, baptize them in the name of the Father and the Son and the Holy Sprit"*. (Matt 28: 19)

The following story "What about Bob?" would explain the Trinity in simple terms: "One day a man walked into my office, he was an electrical contractor interested to bid electrical work, an African American, around 35 years of age. First he greeted me saying "Hello brother", my name is Bob. I replied Hello Bob, what I can do for you? He explained his interest to obtain information to bid a project. Later he asked me: "are you a Muslim?" I replied no, "I was born in Egypt from a Coptic Orthodox Christian family, my ancestors are Christians for almost 2000 years. Saint Mark the Evangelist (the writer of the Gospel of Mark in the Bible) had preached Christianity in Egypt in the year 70 A.D." He then made a connection and said: "from Egypt! I love Egypt, this is in Africa from where my ancestors had come to America", I asked him the same question: "are you a Muslim?" He proudly said: "yes I am, I was born Christian but converted to Islam, when I was young I used to go to Church, I even was an altar boy." I asked, "when and what motivated you to be a Muslim?" He replied, "it was four years ago; when a friend explained to me the religion of Islam, I went to the Mosque and was convinced to accept Islam. I had difficulty to understand how Jesus can be the Son of God? I could not understand the Holy Trinity and found Islam a straightforward religion to call God is One, God had no son, and do not need a mediator to intercede in our behalf between Him and us; this never made sense to me."

After a moment of silence had lapsed, I asked Bob, "do you have children?" He answered, I have two boys; they are 12 and 10 years old. I asked, "Do you love your children?" He replied, "Of course I love them." I asked: "How much?" He looked at me and said, "As much as you can imagine". I asked again, "If one of your boys disobeyed you, he did not listen to your advice, he did not follow your directions, and he foolishly went against your will, what would you do?" He said, "I will discuss the issues with him, see what I can do to help, and I may even see the need to punish him for his wrong doing". I said, "Do you do such act out of your love and care for him?" He replied "certainly". I continued, "If he revolted against you and ran away, do you seek him? Do you remain to love him?" He said, "This will break my heart, but I will continue loving him."

I said, "If your beloved son, while he is away got himself in more trouble, he then realized that he made an awful mistake and cried for your help, what you would do?" I continued, naturally out of your love, you will do any thing in your power to save your son, he nodded, saying yea, I said, "isn't this exactly what God; our heavenly Father did for us? We are His beloved children, it happened that we did not listen to his words, we did not do his will, we disobeyed his commandments and we strayed away going after our wishes. Our heavenly Father loves every one of his children, much more than your love to your boys. Our heavenly father wishes every one of us and all people to do his will and be saved, He always seek man to come back to him, he sent the prophets and through his deep love he finally decided to come to us, so He incarnated in the person of Jesus Christ and appeared to us as a man who spoke our language. He redeemed us to our Father who art in heaven". Bob was silent and listing with saying no comment.

I continued saying, Bob, let me tell you how to understand the mystery of the Holy Trinity; "The Bible says that God created man on his image, so we look alike our father who art in heaven. Sin of Adam and Eve caused separation from their heavenly Father; their bodies became visible and suffered under the authority of Satan. Man has a visible body, a soul and a spirit. Your body is visible, it configures your figure, the soul cannot be seen, it is the person in you that relates to the mind and logic, it controls and directs your body as long as you are alive. The spirit is the third person in you that cannot be seen, it separates mankind from animal kind, it is that person who provides imagination, innovation, and relates directly to your heavenly father." The three are equal and united in one entity.

I continued, "The three persons in you are the Body, the Soul and the Spirit, they form three persons in one, exactly like the Son, the Father and the Holy Spirit, all together are one God. Sin had separated us from God and as long as we live on this earth, God in His Glory is not visible to us. God's righteousness and judgment had passed on Adam and Eve; the judgment is inherited and passed to the seed of mankind. No one can see God in His Glory and live, so because we cannot see God in his Glory, He through His own will and deep love to His children, descended and appeared in the flesh through the person of Jesus Christ who is same and equal to the person of the heavenly Father and to the person of the Holy Spirit. The three persons are one God. The difference between Jesus and us is that Jesus was born alike His father in every thing. He is without sin or sinless, He is Holy, He is Righteous and he is Alive from the very beginning to the end of time, He is equal to his father who art in heaven,. Jesus became a man like us in every thing except sin which separates us from our heavenly father."

I asked Bob, "If God in his absolute power and by His own will decided to appear in the flesh to become a man; so you can see him and talk to you (man to man); would you object and reject him?" He said, "of course not." I continued, "if God the man decided in His absolute power and by His own will to offer himself as a sacrifice or ransom in order to redeem you and to set you free you from the grip of Satan, is this act will be a degradation of God's greatness and authority?" Bob looked at me with teardrops in his eyes and he said nothing.

At this moment, I said, "Believe it, Bob, God loves you and wants you back. God may have sent you here today to hear this message." Bob looked to his watch, stood up and looked at me with more teardrops in his eyes and said, "Mr. Abdelmalek, I thank you, I have been enlightened today, you helped me to understand and clear up matters that troubled me for long time." I asked him to always pray and give glory and thanks to our Lord Jesus Christ. He shook my hand in a very sincere way and left in a hurry for his own business.

Two days later, Bob called me expressing appreciation and asked if I would see him again, I replied, "Surely, any time." This was the last time I heard from Bob. I never saw him again, but he remained vivid in my mind and sometimes I remember him and wonder, what about Bob?"

"The word Trinity is composed of two parts "Tri" meaning three and "Unity" meaning One, thus Tri Unity = Trinity, is a term acknowledging what the Bible reveals about God the Father, God the Son and God the Holy Spirit is One God"

25

GOD IS LOVE

*"There is no fear in love, but perfect love casts out
fear, for fear has to do with punishment, and who
fears is not perfected in love" (1 John 4:18).*

G od's love towards mankind hardly can be found in the Quran;
perhaps the best verse in the Quran, which contains this
injunction, is this one:

Muhammad said, *"If ye love Allah, follow me, Allah will love you
and forgives your sins"* (Quran 3:31). Muhammad asked the people
who love Allah to follow him so Allah forgives their sins. The love is
here functioned with the need of forgiveness of their sins, motivated by
fear and conditional to obtaining forgiveness as a reward of their love.

The Quran also says that Allah loves who do good, *"Spend your
wealth for the cause of Allah, and be not cast yourselves in ruin, and do
good deeds, Allah loves the beneficent"* (Quran 2:135), here again, Allah's
love is conditional to give your wealth for his cause.

Throughout the Quran, we can read that Allah loves those who
do good deeds and punishes those who do bad deeds, approval and
disapproval, reward and punishment, paradise and hell, and so on.

The kind of love relationship between God and mankind similar to that between a loving father and his own children is not revealed in the Quran. The concept of fatherly hood of God is not known in Islam, while in the Bible it is common to call God our Father. No such exalted title is found in the Quran, there is no manifestation of God's love towards mankind; such expression of glorious love cannot be found any where in the Quran. In the Quran, there is no sign for mutual love between God and man except that come out of fear. One of the praising Ninety Nine names of Allah is the name " Al Wadud" or the loving, However, this word does not imply the depth of God's love such as found in the infinite love expression of the Biblical declaration "God is Love" (John 4:8). Moreover, in the Quran there is no expression of love between the Almighty God and man, this is affirmed by AL-Gazzali, a great theologian of Muslim history, saying "God remains above the feeling of love", "love and mercy are desired in respect of their fruit and benefit and not because of empathy feeling". In other words, God has control to give love or mercy to whoever he wishes, man had no privileges, but the emphases are Allah's. God's Mercy for forgiveness is an act of love towards man and is a reward for doing good deeds. The fear from God's wrath and the uncertainty of his forgiveness is expressed throughout the Quran.

Allah of Islam is entirely different than the God known to the Christians. The difference lies hidden in the divinity of Allah. Allah of Islam is comprehensible and unapproachable. He is incredibly great and beyond the scope of intellect, he was not begotten nor beget, none is equal to him. Therefore, the birth of Jesus by Mary is through the will of God, but cannot be called the Son of God; the Muslims abhor this as an unthinkable sensual degradation of Allah.

In Islam Allah is described to be fearful and merciful at the same time, for this reason crucifixion represents an attack on God's sovereignty. Allah needs no sacrifice and no mediator to reconcile mankind to him, because he forgives and punishes whoever and whenever he wants. This concept of Allah's absolute dictatorship is the primary difference between the Muslims and the Christians. So the thought that God the Father appeared in the flesh through His only begotten Son, died for the forgiveness of our sins, out of His love to save mankind is unthinkable in Islam.

A Christian believer has no fear of God's wrath, but only the knowledge of his love. Jesus Christ said to his own disciples *"The Father himself loves you"* (John 16:27). The Day of Judgment will instead be a day of glory for a true Christian.

Let us see more fully what God has done to express his love for us so that we may know the fact that He is indeed our father and learn how He made it possible for this love to be mutual between Him and his children.

The Bible gives such manifestation of God's love. Indeed the greatest possible expression that man could ever expect from God is in the following verses of the Bible; the revelation of God's love is fully set out:

"Beloved let us love one another, for love is of God, and who loves is born of God and knows God. He, who does not love, does not know God, for God is love, so that we might live through him. In this is love, not that we loved God but that he loved us and sent his son to be the expiation for our sins. Beloved, if God so loved us we also ought to love one another. No man has ever seen God; if we love one another, God abides in us and his love is perfected in us" (1 John 4:7-11).

In these verses, it is clear that God's love of mankind is unconditional and is not as Al-Gazzali; one of the most famous Muslim scholars; suggested that it is " Fruit and benefit." One can safely say that more is said about God's love of mankind is included in these four verses of the Bible than in the entire book of the Quran.

What a magnificent act of God to manifest his love in such a way? Many of us could not imagine or understand, it is simply this *"In this is love, not that we love God, but that he loved us and sent his Son to be expiation of our sins"* (1 John 4:10)

No greater proof of God's love can be given to mankind than this, that God the Father out of his love sacrifices his only begotten son Jesus Christ, who is pure without sin, as his Father is, to die on the cross to redeem us to himself.

How many of us understand the depth of this love? When God asked Abraham to sacrifice his beloved son, Isaac, to test his love, Abraham unconditionally obeyed God out of his love, he would give God all things. Because of God's love to Abraham, He provided a lamb for him to sacrifice.

This is precisely what God did out of His infinite love for us; he sacrificed his only begotten son Jesus Christ for forgiveness of our sins. *"He who did not spare his own son but gave him up for us all, will he not give us all things with him?"*(Romans 8:32)

As Abraham accompanied his beloved son up to the mountain, and as the son willingly obeyed the father and carried a load of fire wood for his sacrifice on the alter of God, similarly, God himself sacrificed his only begotten Son as an offering for the redemption of our sins. The son willingly obeyed the father to the end and carried the cross to his own crucifixion. What kind of love could have motivated such an act? The answer can be summed by the following verse: *"For God so loved the world that he scarified his only son, that whoever believe in him should not perish but have eternal life."* (John 3:16)

Nothing else, but love could have endured the cross with all its horrors. Here we have a visible expression of God's love in the gift of His Son; he has given a full manifestation of the depth of his love towards us. *"God shows his love for us while we were yet sinners, Christ died for us"* (Romans 5:8) *"In this the love of God was manifest among us, that God sent his only son in the world that we might love through him"* (1 John 4:9)

It is not surprising that the Quran has so little to say about God's love, when it denies that God gave his only begotten Son to redeem us from our sins. The Quran denies the greatest manifestation of God's love that could ever have been given to us.

It may be worthy to say that the word love has appeared only 69 times in the Quran, mostly used for man's love of things, human love, Allah's love to those who care for cleanness, who are patient, who trust in him, who do not sin, who act justly, who give the poor, who fights for his sake and also in the negative use of the word love in the meaning that Allah does not love, will punish and set stray those who resist his messenger, those who befriend the infidels, and those who love the life of this world more than the hereafter. Following are some examples of the use of the word love found in the Quran:

"Those who love the life of this world more than the thereafter, who hinder from the path of Allah and seek therein crooked ways, they are stray by long distance." (Quran 14:3)

"This because they love the life of this world better than the hereafter and Allah will not guide those who reject faith." (Quran 16:107)

"Nay, but ye love the fleeting life." (Quran 75:20)

"As to those, they love the fleeting life and put away behind them a day hard." (Quran 76:27)

"And ye love wealth with moderate love." (Quran 89:20)

"And violent is he in his love of wealth..." (Quran 100:8)

"Compare the above theme of the use of the word "love" found in the Quran and Ahadith of the Prophet Muhammad to using of the same word of love in the Bible. Jesus Christ made it clear that we are the children of God, and taught us when we pray to say "Our Father who Art in heavens" He said fear not, rejoice and do his commandments out of love, therefore, we will be set free from fear of God's wrath because we are his beloved children."

26

GOD'S SALVATION

O People! Muhammad said, "Do not claim to be the offspring of other than your fathers, as it is a disbelief that you claim to be the offspring of other than your real father." Then He said, " Do not praise me excessively as Jesus the Son of Mary was praised, but call me Allah's slave and His Apostle" The Quran also affirms that Jesus, Son of Mary, was born without the seed of a man or of an earthly father, but was born from the spirit of Allah (God). On the other hand, Muhammad is known to be the son of Abdul- Allah bin Abu-Talib. It is also well known that a new born baby male is usually named after his father's family name to become known as the son of so & so. In the Quran, Jesus is the only person that is named after the name of His Mother; the Son of Mary. Also Mary is the only woman that was ever mentioned in the Quran by her name, described to be the purest of all women ever created in the entire World. On the other hand the Quran denies that Jesus had a father! The Christians believe that God the father, and Jesus is the Son of God.

In the Torah as well as in the Quran, sacrificing by shedding blood is known to be a Godly commandment as offering for forgiveness of sins. The Jews celebrate the Passover by sacrificing a lamb, commemorating their deliverance from bondage. The Muslims sacrifice a sheep for Eid-Al-Adha (Feast of Sacrifice) commemorating Abraham's sacrifice of his son Ishmael. These offerings are for forgiveness of sins through blood shed of sinless sacrificial. Muslims are taught to sacrifice their lives for the cause of spreading Islam in the name of Allah (for sake of Allah); they are promised forgiveness of their sins and earn rewards in Paradise. If Allah calls upon his servants, who are yet sinners to die for his sake, why it is unacceptable that God could offer his only begotten Son whom born sinless through his Holy Spirit, to die for forgiveness of sins and salvation of mankind including Muslims themselves.

The sacrificial of Jesus Christ is an act of God for forgiveness of sins for God's conciliation with Adam and his children. On the cross, Jesus, the son of man, who is sinless, divine and eternal, has paid the ransom in our behalf to satisfy God's judgment namely our eternal death.

Through this Godly act, we have the opportunity to be saved from the eternal death and to be freed from the slavery of Satan; simply because:

- Man's nature is weakness and he repeatedly continue to sin, repentance is the first step to change his ways, his behavior and thoughts.

- Repentance alone is not enough for forgiveness of sins. If repentance could keep man sin no more, what about his previous sins and the original inherited sin?

- Jesus Christ is the only man who is divine, eternal and without sin, God out of His deep love to mankind offered his only begotten son as a sacrificial for forgiveness of sins. The man Jesus did his father's will, willingly and with complete obedience.

- Sacrificial of Jesus Christ provides unlimited sacrifice that was necessary for salvation of the whole human race. No other sacrificial will be enough to satisfy the unlimited judgment against man. No salvation can be achieved without accepting Jesus Christ; He said: *"I am the Way, the Truth and the Life."* Those who reject and refuse Jesus Christ; as their personal savior and Lord; cannot understand the divine secret that God revealed to his children in the person of Jesus Christ.

- The confusion of Muslims about the resurrection of Jesus Christ stems from Muhammad's rejection of Jesus' crucifixion, although Muhammad confirmed in the book of Quran the divine inspiration of the Bible about Jesus:

- His virgin's birth through the Spirit of God;

- His sinless life;

- His divinely authoritative teaching;

- His miracles;

- His ascension;

- And His second coming.

Prophet Muhammad rejected Jesus' own claim to be the Son of God and Savior of mankind; he rejected his death and eventual resurrection; his rejection is based on unproved claim regarding the authenticity of the Bible. On the other hand, Muhammad revealed in the Quran that his message is based on the witness of the previous scriptures saying: *"If you were in doubt as what we have revealed unto you, then ask those who have been reading the Book (the Bible) before you. The truth has indeed come to you from thy Lord"* (Quran 10:94)

The scriptures tells us that Jesus offered himself as the Lamb of God for forgiveness of our sins and for salvation of mankind, he was crucified, died on the cross, resurrected from the dead and ascended into heaven.

After Resurrection of Jesus Christ, God extended his genuine love into our hearts through his Holy Spirit that dwelt in his disciples and that is given to every one who accepts Jesus Christ as his own Savior and Lord, we then become God's children and we are given the right to call him "Our Father who Art in Heaven".

This principal of our adoption as children of God through Jesus Christ and our experience of being God's children through the Holy Spirit is the same eternal, intimate communion that God the Father, and Jesus Christ the Son, has shared from all eternity. As Jesus called upon his Father in heaven, so we through his love and grace we can have intimate relationship with God.

What can man offer to God in return for such unlimited love? Can he give anything in return to compare with it, can we honestly believe that we can merit favor with Him through our own works and hearted feeble religious efforts? God does not want from us our pilgrimages, our prayers, our religious devotions and other various ecclesiastical duties mixed through and through with evil that we think and do every day.

We cannot possibly obtain God's forgiveness by anything we do by our own account. While we casually over look sins we commit, scorn utterly the love revealed to us and repeatedly continue to commit more sins.

The Father wants none of your efforts, He wants you to become his child and to love him with all your heart, soul and mind, then and only then, your good works or religious good deeds will be the fruits of your love and of your intimate relation with God.

It is worthy to note that if there is any one name missing of the praising Ninety-Nine names of Allah listed in the Quran; it is the name "OUR FATHER".

The Quran promises no certainty of forgiveness to those who offer religious works with the hope of obtaining God's approval and forgiveness, their efforts are wrapped in multitude of sins that they commit every day and cannot possibly merit his approval?

The Bible shows us a better and more certain way of salvation; turn away from our own works and trust in Jesus Christ to obtain forgiveness of our sins and win salvation that God freely offered to us. Will you rather turn to him who can save your soul? Would you reach out for salvation through believing in Jesus Christ who gave himself to die on the cross for forgiveness of your sins? Would you receive the Holy Spirit to help you follow His commandments, know that you are a child of God and that He is your heavenly Father?

❧

"That which we have seen and heard we proclaim also to you, so that you may have fellowship with us, and our fellowship is with the Son

Jesus Christ." (1 John 1:3)

❧

27

CHRIST HAS RISEN

The work of salvation was not entirely completed when Jesus Christ died on the cross. When Jesus cried on the cross *"It is finished"* (John 19:30), He was not referring to his work of salvation and redemption, but referring only to that aspect that involved his humiliation and suffering on the cross. The work of redemption had not yet come, but was to begin just three days later when He victoriously arose from the dead.

The Bible tells us the detailed events that confirm the resurrection of Jesus Christ. Three days after the crucifixion and the death of Jesus Christ on the cross, He resurrected and appeared to Mary Magdalene, then He appeared to his disciples, while they were in hiding afraid and terrified of the out come of Jesus' ministry. "Then the same day at evening, beginning the first day of the week, when the doors were shut where the disciples were assembled, in fear of the Jews, Jesus came and stood in the midst, and said to them *"Peace be with you"*, *When He had said this, He showed them His hands and His side. Then the disciples were glad when they saw the lord"* (John 20: 19- 20)

They were glad but terrified, so Jesus said to them again: *"Peace to you! As the Father has sent Me, I also send you. And when He had said this, He breathed on them, and said to them "Receive the Holy Spirit,* (John 20:21-22), by this appearance Jesus affirmed his Ministry and his disciple's work to come.

Thomas, one of the twelve disciples was not with them when Jesus came. The other disciples therefore said to him, *"We have seen the Lord".* So he said to them, *"Unless I see in His hands the print of the nails, and put my hand into his side (to feel the wound), I will not believe"* (John 20: 24-25).

After eight days, His disciples were again inside and Thomas was with them. Jesus came, the doors being shut, and stood in the midst, and said, *"Peace to you!"* Then He said to Thomas, *"Reach your finger here, and look at my hands: and reach your hand here, and put it into my side, do not be unbelieving, but believing."* And Thomas answered and said to Him, "My Lord and my God!" Jesus said to him, *"Thomas, because you have seen me, you have believed. Blessed are those who have not seen and yet have believed"* (John 20: 26-29).

After these appearances Jesus appeared again to a number of disciples at the sea of Tiberias. He then appeared to Simon Peter and Nathanael of Cana in Galilee, the sons of Zebedee, and to others of His disciples.

The resurrection of Jesus Christ was necessary to complete the redemption process. To understand the significance of the resurrection of Jesus, we must understand the nature of the penalty imposed upon sinners and upon the sinful world by God's righteous Judgment. It can be summarized with the word death: *"the wages of sin is death"* (Romans, 6:23), The judgment of spiritual death of all human beings is inherited as a result of Adam's Sin.

Through His Resurrection from the dead, Jesus Christ made available to us the power to reverse the spiritual death and restore us to life. Jesus Said:

"In this is the will of my Father that every one who looks on the Son and believes in him should have eternal life, and I will raise him upon the last day" (John 6:38-40).

During his earthly ministry, Jesus made many claims that seemed outrageous coming from a mere carpenter from Nazareth. Jesus claimed that He is the Christ, the Son of God (Matt 16:16-20), that He is one with the Father (John 10:30), that He has authority to forgive sins (Matt 9:2-6).

All these claims were put to the test when Jesus was put to death, and proven to be true when he arose victoriously from the dead.

"He was declared the son of God with power by the resurrection from the dead" (Roman 1:4). Jesus said: *"I am the bread of life, whoever comes to me shall not hunger, and whoever believes me shall never thirst."* (John; 6: 35)

Jesus Christ's resurrection had defeated Satan; the Son of God came to our world to destroy the works of the devil. Shortly before crucifixion, Jesus warned his disciples that a final battle with the ruler of the world (Satan) was approaching. Jesus said: *"Now is the judgment of this world; now will the ruler of this world (Satan) be cast out. And I, when I am lifted up from the earth, I will draw all people to myself."* (John 12:31-32). Satan was defeated through the crucifixion and resurrection of Jesus Christ.

Saint Paul said: *"For our sake He made him to be sin that knew no sin, so that in him we might become the righteousness of God"* (2 Corinthians 5:21)

The divine power of resurrection that brought Jesus back to life and let him free from death, absolutely devastated the forces of evil for all times, the risen Christ declared *"I am... the living one, and I was dead and behold, I am alive forevermore, and I have the Key of death and Hades."* (Rev, 1:17-18)

Jesus not only devastated the forces of evil for all times. He delivered us from the domination of Satan and gave us power that is greater than Satan's. *"Little children, you are from God and have overcome them, for greater is who is in you than he who is in the world"* (1 John 4:4)

Believing in the power of Jesus' resurrection enables us to defeat Satan and to crush him under our feet. Resurrection is the beginning of a new creation. Before resurrection, man suffered the effects of sin, and death, but resurrection fulfilled God's promise of salvation, the promise of new creation. Jesus Said *"Behold I am making all things new"* (Rev. 21:5).

Resurrection was the first event of its kind ever. The glorified body of Jesus was first instance of the new order from which death is forever defeated. In that spiritual sense of life, *"There will be no longer any death, nor any thing related to it. No mourning, or crying or pain"* (Rev 21:4).

Resurrection is the turning point for a new creation or new eternal age. It is the very foundation which all life now depends, in which we sustain living in the midst of a dying world, and offers the hope for the new creation to come.

Saint Paul said *"For as by one man (Adam) came death, by one man (Jesus) has come also the resurrection of the dead, for as in Adam all die, so also in Christ shall all be made alive"* (1 Cor 15:21-22).

Resurrection of Jesus Christ is the basis of the Christian faith in the promises of salvation, believing in God's power to raise the dead to life again, the promise of spiritual and bodily resurrection.

Through Jesus Christ's resurrection, we are born again to a living hope.

"Christ has risen, He is truly risen. Resurrection gives life to all people who believe in Him. Therefore, if you believe, you become no longer a slave but a son and heir of God through Christ. Put your trust in Him, for in that He himself has suffered, being tempted, He is able to aid those who are tempted."

28

THE PERFECT PEACE

In an effort to defend Islam, many Muslim scholars speak of Islam as a religion of peace and not of violence. They say that the non-Muslims misunderstand the Quran verses about Jihad and the conduct of war in Islam. They promote that violence and bloodshed are permitted only to defend the Muslims from attacks by non-Muslims.

"Keep fighting against them until mischief ends and the way prescribed by Allah prevail. But, if they desist, then know that hostility is only against the wrong-doers." (Quran 2: 193)

"Fight against those who fight against you in the way of Allah, but do not transgress, for Allah does not love transgressors." (Quran 2:190)

It is obvious that in the Quran many commandments are written for holding peace among Muslims themselves (House of peace), and for fighting the unbelievers (House of war). Muslim extremists justify the fighting or Jihad against those who reject Islam as being ordered by Allah. On the other hand, moderate Muslims say that the Quran commands no compulsion in Islam and reject the extreme Muslims misinterpretation of the Quran regarding the commands for Jihad.

Moderate Muslims say that Islam means peace, the Hebrew word for peace is "*Shalom*", in Arabic language it is "*Salaam*", and the word Islam is driven from the word Salaam or peace. When Muslims pronounce the name of the prophet Muhammad, they must follow his name by saying "Peace and blessings be upon Him". The common Muslim greeting words are "*Al –Salaam- Alykum*" which means "Peace is upon you." Other than greetings, the word peace cannot be found in the Quran outside the context of the acts of fighting and war. The Quran does not shy from advocating war and violence against the infidels and the unbelievers who resist Islam. Jihad is declared against those who reject Islam for their own religion and against those who resist to be ruled by the Islamic laws. *"But if the enemy incline towards peace, do thou (also) incline towards peace"* (Quran 8:61)

It is said: sometimes force has to be used to maintain peace; of course this requires fighting and bloodshed. The great Philosopher, George Bernard Shaw said once praising the works of the Prophet Muhammad: " If a man like Muhammad were to assume the dictatorship of the modern world, He would succeed in solving its problems that would bring it the much needed peace and happiness." One can imagine what the outcome would be if the world is ruled under the shadow of the sword!

It is apparent that Islamic and the Christian ideologies are on the opposite sides of the issue of peace. In the Christian belief, the word peace is associated with God himself; it is only in Christ that we can have true peace. Having peace with God through our Savior Jesus Christ, and living a life faithful to Him, will allow us to be at peace with others and ourselves.

When Jesus was brought before the Roman Governor Pontius Pilate, Pilate asked Jesus: Are you a King? Jesus answered, *"...My kingdom is not of this world. If my kingdom were of this world, then my servant's would fight, so that I should not be delivered to the Jews. But now is my kingdom not from Here."* (John 18:33- 36)

The peace that Christ brought is primarily spiritual peace from and with God. The Gospel teaches that it is the duty of the Christian to bring and spread peace among men's hearts through accepting Jesus Christ our Lord, the king of Peace.

Jesus said: *"Blessed are the Peace Makers; for they shall be called Sons of God"* (Matt. 5:9)

The term Peace Maker here implies not only making peace between nations at war or fighting each other, but also making peace with those who are hurt, have hardships or troubled because of people's lack of love to one another, they are not at peace at their families or at work and every where.

Jesus Said to his disciples: *"These things I have spoken to you that in me you may have peace. In the world you will have tribulation, but be of good cheer, I have overcome the world"* (John 16:33). Saint Paul said; *"But the fruit of the sprit is love, joy, peace, long suffering, gentleness, goodness, faith, meekness, temperance, against such there is no law."* (Gal. 5:22-23)

The perfect peace is the inward peace, the peace of conscience, the peace of God's rule in your heart. The peace of the truth, the peace of honesty, the peace of justice, the peace of purity, the peace of love, and the peace of goodness.

Once a Christian exclaimed: "What would Jesus do in response to the Islamic terrorist acts? Can we picture Jesus and his disciples running a bomb squadron to crush the evil system they had to deal with terrorism? They did confront the powers of evil, but with radically different way. It is right that those responsible for these massive acts of inhumanity are aught to be called to account, but Jesus' resurrection gives hope, brings life out of death, strength out of weakness, and peace out of chaos.

Jesus teaching the multitude in the sermon of the mount said: " *You have heard it said "An eye for an eye, and a tooth for a tooth",* but I say to you *"Resist not the evil one."* you have heard it said *"Love your neighbor and hate your enemy"* but I say to you *"Love your enemies"* (Matt 5:38-44)

Peace is the fruit of trusting in God through our Savior and Lord Jesus Christ; and by living a life justified by Faith, Humility, Love, Righteousness and Patience.

Faith in God the Father and in His Son Jesus Christ is essential in the lives of the Christian believers. This faith should be founded on the truth of God's word and should be demonstrated by the works we do. Christ dwells in our hearts, sanctifies us, purifies us, justifies us, gives us access to God's grace, makes us righteous and leads us to victory that overcomes the world to have eternal life. *"Therefore, having been justiJied by faith, we have peace with God through our Lord Jesus Christ"* (Romans 5:1)

Peace is the fruit of faith in God, through faith we gain safety and comfort. *"By faith, Noah being warned by God of things not seen as yet, moved with trust, prepared an ark on dry land to save his House and every kind of living soul lived on the earth."* (Hebrews 11: 7)

While pride has always condemned by God, the Bible shows that humility is one trait that should be characteristic of God's people. Those who are humble will be blessed and exalted by God. Jesus said: *"Therefore whoever humbles himself as this little child is the greatest in the Kingdom of Heaven"* (Matt: 18:4)? *"Therefore he says,"* God resists the *proud, but gives grace to the humble. Humble yourselves in the sight of the Lord, and He will lift you up."* (James 4:6, 10)

The Christian should love God and other people. Christ demands that we love all men, even our enemies. The kind of love that a Christian is to have must be displayed by what he does. " *You have heard that it was said, you shall love your neighbor and hate your enemy, but I say to you, Love your enemies, bless those who curse you, do good to those who hate you, that you may be sons of your Father in heaven*". (Matt 5: 43)

"Love suffers long and is kind; love does not envy, love does not parade itself, is not puffed; does not behave rudely, does not seek its own, is not provoked, thinks no evil; does not rejoice in iniquity, but rejoices in the truth; bears all things, believes all things, hopes all things, endures all things, love never fails." (1 Cor. 13: 4-8)

Selfless love brings healing to hurting and damaged emotions, restoration of relations, revival of peace and spiritual growth. The light of the Holy Spirit of God in you shines through love. *"And let the peace of God rule in your hearts to which also ye are called in one body; and be ye thankful."* (Col. 3:15)

Most people think that love and peace are optional, but they are not, they are mandatory for us to be called the children of God. Patience, Long suffering, forbearance, and perseverance are some terms that are used interchangeably with love to achieve peace. God has been profoundly patient with us and tells us to be patient as He fulfills our needs.

The Bible teaches us not to harm any one but do good, be holy, meek and compassionate, forgive one another, do every thing that imitate what Jesus Himself would do if He is in your place. If you do all things in Christ's name, His Spirit will dwell in you and he will rule over your heart and every aspect of your life. You should be thankful that in Jesus Christ, you are no longer a part of the violent nature of this world; you may be affected by it, but you are not part of it because the peace of Jesus Christ rules in your heart.

Inward peace is the fruit of the righteousness of a person that trusts God, it makes a person acceptable to God and God is revealed in the good works he does. When Jesus Christ was preparing to depart from this world, He told His disciples: *"But the Helper, the Holy spirit, whom the Father will send in My Name, He will teach you all things, and bring to you remembrance all that I said to you. Peace I leave with you; my peace I give to you: not as the world gives do I give to you. Let not your hearts be troubled, nor let it be fearful."* (John 14: 26-27)

Jesus teaching the multitude in the Sermon on the Mount said: *"Blessed are those who hunger and thirst for righteousness, for they shall be Jilled"* (Matt. 5:6)

"He who practices righteousness is righteous, just as He (God) is righteous. He who sins is of the devil, for the devil has sinned from the beginning, for this purpose the Son of God was manifested, that He might destroy the works of the devil" (1 John 3: 7-8)

"But you O' man of God, flee these things and pursue righteousness, goodness, with faith, love, patience and gentleness" (Col. 3:12-13)

The Bible tells us a story that one time Jesus was sleeping in a ship of his disciples during a bad stormy weather, his disciples were afraid that the boat would capsize because the wind was strong and the seawaters were high. They awoke Jesus and he rebuked the wind by saying to the wind *"Peace be still"* (Mark 4:39). The wind died down and everything became perfectly in still peace.

Think about it. If Jesus rebuked the wind and the high waters of the sea to bring peace into nature and comfort to his disciples, what about your own troubles, your own ship of life sailing in high waters and strong winds? You are afraid that you may lose control and get deeper into trouble. What you should do? Call on Him, Jesus Christ is He who can give you peace and calm the storm to your safety.

What this means to us? If we allow Jesus Christ to rule on our lives, He promised that in His name, the Holy Spirit will teach us all things. What kind blessing for us to receive this free gift of peace to be with us? Do we accept receiving Him in our hearts and let Him command our lives? If we do, Saint Paul tells us that we would: *"Rejoice always, and in every thing give thanks; for this is God's will for you in Jesus Christ."* Then he adds a caution "Do not quench the Spirit." For the Holy Spirit is the witness to us of the Prince of Peace, and how the Lord wants us to continue live in peace.

Jesus Christ came to bring peace to the whole world, not just to a few self-selected people. He stands by your door and knocks, if you open, he comes in and be with you and you become with Him. Only through Him, you will gain contentment, gain strength, overcome tribulations, and gain tranquility through peace.

Seven Centuries before Jesus Christ, the prophet Isaiah prophesied about Jesus, he wrote: *"For a child will be born to us, a son will be given to us; and the Government will rest on His shoulders; And his name will be called wonderful counselor, mighty God, Eternal Father, Prince of Peace. There will be no end to the increase of His Government for Peace, on the throne of David and over his kingdom, to establish it and to uphold it with justice and righteousness. From then and forevermore, the zeal of the Lord of hosts will accomplish this."* (Isa. 9:6-7).

ରେ

"Jesus' resurrection gives hope, brings life out of death, strength out of weakness and peace out of chaos. Only in Jesus Christ we can have true peace"

ରେ

29

YOU ARE INVITED

Both the Bible and the Quran say that God created man on his own image; this is a great privilege and gives us dignity. Both the Bible and Quran say that Jesus Christ is the only human being born from the Holy Spirit of God with no sin, born from the Virgin Mary without the seed of man, he is the only human who rose from death and ascended into heaven, he is alive!

In other words, Jesus is the eternal word of God was born with the same attributes of God, righteous, without sin, the visible image of God, and the exact representation of his being like God in image and spirit. People often use the phrase: "like father, like son" Jesus Christ was God incarnate, God appeared in the flesh, truly Righteous and Holy." He came down to take our nature and to lift us to take his nature.

So, if God became a man, what we would expect of him?

- To be without sin, or **Sinless**.

- To manifest his supernatural presence in the form of supernatural acts; **Miracles**.

- To live more perfectly than any human ever lived; **Perfect**.

- To speak the greatest words ever spoken: **Holy.**

- To have ever lasting and universal influence: **Eternal**

- To satisfy the spiritual Hunger in humanity, or **Loving.**

- To overcome humanity's most pervasive and feared enemy; conquer **Death.**

- Jesus Christ taught us "Be holy as your heavenly father is holy", like any father who guides and teaches his obedient son, God is working through the Holy Spirit, giving you the desire to obey him and the power to do what pleases Him. God wants his children to grow and to mature in spirit to be holy same as Jesus is Holy.

- Stop and think this over, do not become so well adjusted to your culture in which you comfortably fitted yourself without even thinking. Instead fix your attention on Christ; you will be changed from the inside out. Unlike the culture around you, always dragging you down to its level of immaturity, God brings the best out of you and develops well-formed maturity in you. You must be strong to make a different decision, focus on becoming like Jesus, otherwise, pressing forces such as peers, parents, co-workers and immediate community culture will try to mold you into their image. You will unconsciously sin, and slowly sin will become your habit and a normal way of life because sin is driven by many human weaknesses similar to:

- *Fear:* many people live fearful life, fear of death, fear of punishment, or fear of judgment. Fear-driven people often miss great opportunities and do not live a peaceful live.

- *Need for approval:* many are driven by the expectations to satisfy a religious leader, some worried by what others may think, or feel secured to follow the majority and maybe controlled by the opinions of others.

- *Anger*: many do not accept others, loose their peace of mind and cannot think rationally, they unconsciously act violently and sinfully.

- *Need of things*: many let the earthly needs for the body, food, cloth, shelter, sex and money to divert their focus and their trust fades away from God, the source of every thing good you may need.

- *Ambition*: many are unhappy with their life, pressured by their peers, and loose hope trying to reach beyond their capabilities. You may have reformed your life in many ways. You may have had religious affections. You may believe in a form of religion rituals, and you may do many good deeds believing that this is the way for your salvation. Nothing, but Jesus Christ that will keep you from being this very moment perish in everlasting death and destruction in a lake of fire.

- The following are known as "The Four Spiritual Laws" defined by William Bright:

- God Loves You, and offers a wonderful plan for your life; *"For God so loved the world, that He gave His only begotten Son, that whoever believes in Him should not perish but have everlasting life"* (John 3:16)

- Man is sinful, and separated from God, therefore, he cannot know and experience God's love and plan for his life *"For all have sinned and fall short of Glory of God"* (Romans 3: 23). Man's sin had separated him from God's Grace, but God's love has bridged the gulf that separated us from him by sending His Son Jesus Christ to die on the Cross- in our place to pay the penalty for our sins.

- Jesus Christ is God's only provision for Man's Salvation. Christ died for our sins…He was buried…He rose again in the third day according to the scriptures… He was seen by Cephas, then by the twelve. After that He was seen by over five hundred. Through Him you know and experience God's love and plan for your life. *"But God demonstrates His own love toward us, in that while we were still sinners, Christ died for us"* (Romans 5:8), (1 Corinthians 15:3-6). Jesus said, *"I am the way, the truth, and the life. No one comes to the Father except through me"* (John 14:6).

- You must have the will to accept Jesus Christ's as your own Savior and Lord; then you will be able to know and experience God's Grace and plan for your salvation. *"But as many as received Him, to them, He gave the right to become children of God, to those who believe in His name"* (John 1:12); *" For by grace you have been saved through faith, and that not of yourselves; it is the gift of God, not of works, lest any one should boast"* (Ephesians 2:8,9); Jesus said *"Behold, I stand at the door and knock, if anyone hears my voice and opens the door, I will come in to him"* (Revelation 3:20).

Jesus knocking on your door

Receiving Jesus Christ involves turning to God from self (Repentance) and trusting Jesus to come into your life, to forgive your sins and to make you the kind of person He wants you to be. It is not enough to just agree intellectually that Jesus Christ is the Son of God, and that He died on the cross for your sins. Jesus Christ said He would come in your life if you open the door and allow him to enter. You would invite Jesus Christ by faith and through prayer, confess your sins and ask Him forgiveness, trust in God's promise, He who knows your heart.

The Bible confirms eternal life to all who receive Jesus Christ; *"And this is the testimony; that God has given us eternal life, and this life is in His Son. He who has the Son has life; he who does not have the Son of God does not have life. These things I have written to you who believe in the name of the Son of God, that you may know that you have eternal life"* (1 John 5:11-13)

On the basis of his promise, you can be certain that Jesus Christ lives in you and that you have eternal life, from the very moment you invite him in, he will not leave you. So once God's promise is fulfilled, you must live by faith (Trust) and pray that He guides you to learn His commandments and to do his will.

So start right now with the following suggested prayer:

"Lord Jesus, I need you, come and stay with me. I thank you for dying on the cross for my sins. I open the door of my life and receive you as my savior and lord. Thank you for forgiving my sins and giving me eternal life. Take control of my life, make me the kind of person you want me to be."

If this prayer expresses the desire of your heart, be sure that Jesus Christ has accepted your prayer. Once you have invited Jesus into your life, the Bible explains that, you become a child of God, receive His Holy Spirit and begin a great adventure for which God prepared for your eternal life.

Can you think of anything more wonderful that could happen to you than receiving Jesus Christ? Would you like to experience a personal relationship with God? Start to do what Jesus Christ taught his disciples:

"And when you pray, you shall not be like the hypocrites, for they love to pray standing in the synagogues and on the corners of the streets, that they may be seen by men. Assuredly, I say to you, they have their reward. But you when you pray go into your room, and when you have shut your door, pray to your father who sees in secret will reward you openly. And when you pray, do not use vain repetitions as the heathen do, because He knows the things you have need of before you ask Him. In this manner", therefore, pray:

"Our Father who art in heaven, Hallowed be your name, your kingdom come, your will be done, on earth as it is in heaven. Give us this day our daily bread. And forgive our debts, as we forgive our debtors, and not lead us into temptation, but deliver us from the evil one, for yours is the kingdom and the power and the glory forever. Amen." (Matthew 5:5- 13).

Accepting Jesus Christ in your life is the first step of your spiritual growth. A life of faith will enable you to trust God increasingly with every detail of your life, you will experience and practice the word GROWTH:

G -"Go to God in Prayer daily" (John 15:7) R- "Read God's word daily (Acts 17:11), begin with the Gospel of John." O- "Obey God moment by moment." W- "Witness for Christ by your life and words." (Matthew 4:19; John 15:8).

T- "Trust God for every thing in your life." (1 Peter 5:7). H - "Holy Spirit- allow the Holy Spirit to control and empower your daily life." (Galatians 5:16-17; Acts 1:8)

Now, If you do not yet belong to a church, do not wait to be invited, take the initiative, look to have fellowship in a good church, call a Pastor of a near-by church where Jesus Christ is honored and His Word is preached. Start this week, and make plans to attend regularly.

cð

"By accepting God's gift of Jesus Christ as your lord, you just started your most exciting life journey to salvation and eternity. You swapped the sword for the cross, hate for love, ignorance for knowledge, bondage for freedom and death for life. Only our lord Jesus Christ is He who acts through his church and the Holy Spirit to guide you to do the will of God. You will take the image of Christ; will be a child of God, Chosen vessel, a holy temple and a foundation of holiness for all those who approach you to be a reason for their salvation."

cð

AFTERWORD

The thought that God is a Father and that He offered his only Son, out of His love, to save the corrupted world is not only strange for a Muslim, but also ridiculous, if not blasphemous. Instead a distant mighty and great dictator-God worshipped and feared. Every assertion of the nearness of God and his fatherly care is regarded and remains as always far from his creatures. He, who says that God revealed Himself in the man Jesus, is regarded as a liar and seducer.

Allah dictated the Quran to Muhammad word by word so that the nearly unconscious prophet spoke the Arabic verses as a powerless tool of a spirit. Muslims regard his prophecy as conclusion of all revelations in which the highest wisdom and deepest knowledge are presented to mankind. Muslims are not allowed to critically discuss or argue the contents of the revealed verses. They believe that all revelations were given by God, and only must be received passively, accepted obediently, and kept faithfully, but never opened for discussion, criticized or subjected to change.

Islam's influence on thinking is dictated by the fact that the Quran in Arabic rhyme is memorized completely or partially by heart without being rightfully understood. No man has the right to interpret the Quran with his own intellect or to apply interpretation to new situations. Only Allah through His messenger Muhammad alone can do that. Therefore the concept of abrogation is known in Islam (Muhammad's later revelation cancels a previous revelation). Muslims are to adhere to volumes of rules of conduct established in the traditions (way of life and sayings) of the Prophet Muhammad. This created a large number of contradictions and became the basis for radicals to hold ground for their extreme views enforcing those radical rules as an indication that freethinking is basically eliminated in Islam.

The tribal and clan type culture is the breeding environments for the radical and terrorist movements. This remains among many of the Arab countries, most of them are now in transition from the clan-controlled society to the free decision of the individual alone. In this tribal and clan culture, when a Muslim does leave his faith, brings great disgrace to his family. He is pressured to leave the family in which he is heavily rooted and anchored to since his birth. Leaving the Muslim faith is a deeper and more sever process than most of us can imagine. It can cause many converts to become solitary, leading to despair and losing hope in life.

When a Muslim comes to Jesus Christ, he is confronted with the most basic sin in Islam, *"whoever setup another God beside Allah, throw him into a severe penalty"* (Quran 50:26), and *"those who reject faith never will their repentance be accepted"* (Quran 3:90). In addition to all the pressures of dogma, logic and family, comes the voice of his own conscience restraining a Muslim from coming to Christ.

Six hundred and twenty years after the death and resurrection of our Lord Jesus Christ, Muhammad rejected Him as his Lord, Son of God and Savior of mankind, and developed an anti-Christ movement. Muslims are brainwashed at a very early stage in life and become immune to accept the spirit of Christ and the teachings of the Gospel, another spirit keeps them captive that could be described as a collective possession of the body and soul.

Often Muslims who come to Jesus Christ try to uphold both sources of revelation as truth, the result of this position is schizophrenia that blooms a mighty and superficial faith, which soon disintegrates.

Modern advances in education, technologies, computer, Internet and satellite broadcasting had created an irresistible upheaval in Islamic culture. The tribal clan type of living is now disintegrating into larger cities, young families now live into smaller apartments in high rise buildings, separated from the clan's system which remains the guardian of the Islamic customs and teachings. Many people are increasingly searching for a new spiritual settlement and internal security like never before.

In the Arab world, when a Muslim comes to Jesus Christ, his deepest roots with his community and family are irreparably broken. He will be persecuted, rejected by his immediate family and feel the shock of emptiness and loneliness in a world that knows no compassion. Fear from violating the Islamic laws in Arab countries in the Middle East prevent the native church leaders from providing aid or support to the new converts to Christ. Certainly, the negative experience of the church in the Middle East is a result and an indication of the terror condition and dictatorship regimes that the church strives to deal with.

The growth of faith becomes active in love and abides in a living hope that needs much time, counseling and living examples. Often a person who is captivated by Islam's spirit only changes through sustained prayer, let him first see your good deeds so he magnifies your Father who Art in heaven. Christ alone can free and change a Muslim. All skills in persuasion to convert a Muslim are of no help, Christ Himself is who liberate, cleanse, revive, and sustain a Muslim in love. The ability of Grace alone to renew creation is the same that overcomes the power of Islam.

When a Muslim reaches the point to ask for guidance and help to come to Christ, he already has experienced severe spiritual struggle, pressured, confused and exhausted, he needs comfort, love and support. A new believer in Christ does not need empty words, but prayers. He needs a warm nest of belonging and a new family or a church to watch over him like a mother that watches and nurses her young child. It takes years of patience while the subconscious of a former Muslim is filled with Christian thoughts. The old spirit must leave, and the new spirit must enter. So if a Muslim becomes a Christian and is later turned back to his old religion, we should blame our little faith, our weak prayers, our deficient love and our missing willingness to sacrifice.

During the early stage of spiritual growth, there is a dangerous phase in which some new believers in Christ turn back to Islam. Many idealize their new faith and imagine pastors and priests to be perfect. When they discover there are flaws in these followers of Christ, they will watch them closely. They may see traces of selfishness, ambition, hard-heartedness, impatience and many other things over which they become discouraged and may cause them to say, "These Christians are not any better than we are." New converts become aware of and shocked by the different denominations and the principles of strange missions, they see that Christians are not united, and every one thinks that his church is holier and better than that of the other. The new believer then quickly finds himself lost, again.

Forgiveness is the key word in relationships with other believers. Humility and self-denial do not begin with the other person, but with oneself. The path of self-denial is the only way to inner growth and the formation of the true church. Some situations may make you vulnerable to temptation, and may cause you to stumble almost immediately. These situations are unique to your weaknesses, you need to identify them and pray for Jesus' help, because Satan surely knows your weaknesses and he is constantly working to get you back in his grip. Saint Peter warns, *"Stay alert. The Devil is poised to pounce, and would like nothing better than to catch you napping"* (1 Peter 5:8).

In conclusion of his ministry, Jesus Christ said to his disciples *"Now that you know these things, you will be blessed if you do them"* (John 13:17). Today God calls you to do his will, He also wants you to be a member of his family, to help others do the same, bring them into his fellowship, help them to grow to maturity and discover how much God loved each one of us that He gave up his only begotten son for our salvation. In the Bible, Saint Paul said, *"For Christ's love compelling us, because we are convinced that one died for all"* (Corinthians 5:14), also he said *"Make the most of your chances to tell others the Good News. Be wise in all your contacts with them"* (Colossians 4:5).

Now, that you have invited Jesus Christ into your life, and have developed your relationship with Him and become a member of his family, what are the blessings you have earned? Following are the top 10 of these blessings:

10. You were a **sinner** and now your sins are **forgiven**.

9. You were **lost** and now you are **found**.

8. You were **possessed** and now you are *freed*.

7. You were **sick** and now you are **healed**.

6. You were **blind** and now you can **see**.

5. You were **troubled** and now you are **contented**.

4. You were **confused** and now you can **understand**.

3. You were **angry** and now you are **Peaceful**.

2. You were full with **hatred** and now you are filled with **love**.

1. You were **dead** and now you are **alive**.

૭๏

As a result of reading this book, if just one person; who maybe you; accept Jesus Christ to earn free salvation, then the book had fulfilled its purpose"

૭๏

GLOSSARY

Abbasid Caliphate: 750-1258 A.D., succeeded the Umayyad Caliphate, the capital was moved from Damascus to Baghdad.

Abdul-Mutalib: Muhammad's Grandfather, he took care of him since his birth until be became six years old.

Abdullah; Muhammad's father, died before his birth.

Abraham: The Prophet, Father of Ishmael and Isaac, Muhammad claimed that Abraham is the first Muslim.

Abrogation: A later revealed verse in the Quran cancels a previous verse concerning a change in Allah's commandments.

Abu Baker: Close friend and companion of Muhammad, one of the first of the converts to Islam, the first Caliph, and the father of Ayisha who was Muhammad's third wife?

Abu Sayyaf Group; An Islamic terrorist group based in Philippines. *Abu Talib*: Uncle of Muhammad, one of the first converts of Islam; His son Ali married Fatima, the youngest daughter of Muhammad. *Ahadith*; Thousands of reports of the sayings and traditions of the prophet Muhammad that was collected and recorded by Muslim Scholars. *Ahl- AL-Dimmah*: Arabic term for the non-Muslims who live under Islamic rule.

Ahl-Al- Kitab: An Arabic Phrase, which means "People of the Book" or the Bible, referring the Jews and Christians.

Ahmadis: An Islamic sect, started in India in the later half of the 19th century by self proclaimed prophet called Mizra Ghulam.

Al- Gama'al Islamia: (Islamic Group), An Islamic extremist militant group based in Egypt.

Al-Aqssa Mosque: An Islamic historic mosque built over the site of the great temple of Solomon. Muslims believe this is the place Muhammad visited during his night journey to heavens.

Al-Bukahri: One of the most trusted Muslim Scholars who recorded the Ahadith or sayings of the Prophet Muhammad.

Al-Gazzali: One of the most trusted Muslim Scholars who recorded the Ahadith or sayings, and of the Prophet Muhammad.

Al-Hussayn: Son of Ali Ibn Abu-Talib, cousin of Muhammad.

Ali-Ibn Abu Talib: First cousin of Muhammad and one of his earliest converts, married Fatima, the youngest daughter of Muhammad, and the fourth Caliph from whom come the Succession of the Shiite's Imams:

Al-Tabari: One of the known Muslim Scholars who recorded the sayings of the prophet.

Amina: Muhammad's mother, died when he was 6 years old.

Alms: charity and giving to the poor and needy. Muslims are obligated to give 2.5% of their income in alms.

Allah: Is an Arabic word for God; in pre-Islam era, Allah was the chief Idol of the Moon (Crescent) god that was worshiped by a Satanic Cult in Jahilliah.

Al-Quaida: Terrorist Islamic Organization led by Osama-bin-Ladin.

Anwar Sadat: Former president of Egypt, assassinated by radical Muslim fundamentalists on October 6, 1979.

Arab Peninsula: The dwelling place for various tribal and nomadic groups, presently known as Saudi Arabia.

Armed Islamic Group: An Islamic terrorist group based in Algeria, the group has been working to overthrow the Algerian regime and replace it with Islamic State.

Arius: An Alexandrian priest who preached that Jesus has two natures, a human nature and a divine nature, which are separate and are not united as one.

Athanasius: An Alexandrian deacon of the Coptic Orthodox Church who opposed the teachings of Arius and defended the Christian faith that Jesus is God who appeared in the flesh. He wrote the Nicene Creed, which is recited throughout the Christian world.

Attaturk, Mustafa Kamal: Turkish leader who abolished the Ottoman Caliphate system in 1922 and established a new secular rule of modern Turkey.

Ayatollah Ruhallah khomeini: Chief Islamic leader of Iran from 1979 to 1989, the name means "Sign and Spirit of Allah"

Ayisha: Muhammad's third wife, daughter of Abu Baker, the first Caliph. She was 9 years old when Muhammad married her.

Ayyubids: A Muslim reign named after Salah Al Din Al-Ayyubi, who defeated the crusaders, He established his rule from Cairo, Egypt. ***Banu Quraizah***: A Jewish tribe that was attacked and defeated by Muhammad's armed followers.

Black Stone; Muslims believe the stone is sacred handed to Abraham by the Angel Gabriel. It is installed in the Corner of the Kaabah.

Buhaira: A Nestorian monk who lived in Basra on a caravan route and had a strong influence on Muhammad.

Burga: A woman's head to toe cover.

Buraq: A miraculous winged horse with human face that took Muhammad in a flight into heavens in a one-night journey known by the "Night Journey".

Byzantine Empire: The Eastern Roman Empire headed by an Emperor that ruled most of the Middle East region.

Caliph: Successor of Muhammad as the spiritual and political leader of the Muslims.

Council of Chalcedon: Convened in year AD, 451 to discuss a dispute about the divine nature of Jesus Christ that caused division of the early Christian Church into the Western Roman Catholic Church and the Eastern Orthodox Church.

Council of Ephesus: Was called in year 381 AD to discuss the disputed teachings of Nestor regarding the divine nature of Jesus Christ.

Council of Niece: Was convened by the Christian Emperor Constantine to resolve a theological dispute started by Alexandrian priest called Arius about the nature of Christ. The council led to the formation of the creed of faith known as the Nicene Creed.

Dajjal: Name of the anti-Christ who will appear at the end of time.

Dome of the Rock: The second most holy place of Islam, Muslims believe it was built on the spot where Muhammad landed in Jerusalem during his Miraculous Night Journey before his ascension into heavens.

El-Lat, Menat and Uzza: Three Pagan idol goddesses that Muhammad revealed the Satanic verses about their intersection powers with Allah. **Fatima**: The youngest daughter of Muhammad by his first wife Kadigah.

Fatwa: Religious decree or legal ruling according to the creed (shidadah), Prayer (salah), Fasting, Alms giving (zakat), and Pilgrimage (Hajj).

Goog and Magoog: Name of the forces that will invade and demolish the Kaabah in the Last Day.

Five Pillars of faith: Are the chief religious duties of Muslims, namely to recite as indivisible part of the Quran and Islamic law.

Hagia Sophia: A Byzantine church in Istanbul, was converted to a mosque.

Hammas; A Palestinian Islamic organization with a military wing based in Gaza Strip and the West Bank known as the Islamic Resistance Movement and known by its attacks against Israel. The organization has succeeded in the general elections of the government of Palestine. Hammas opposed the accord between Israel and the Palestine Liberation Organization (PLO), and continue to reject recognition of the State of Israel.

Hajj: An annual pilgrimage to Mecca, one of the five pillars of the Islamic faith. Hajj is Compulsory for a Muslim once in a lifetime.

Hashim: A clan of the tribe of Quraysh

Hezbullah; Meaning the party of Allah, One of the leading Shiite's religious and political organizations based in Iran and Lebanon.

Hijra: Muhammad's flight from Mecca to Medina

Hijab: Head cover (Scarf), for a Muslim woman to wrap her head and face according to the Islamic law.

Houris: Fabulous maiden of the paradise.

Hussayn: Son of Ali-Ibn AbuTalib, the cousin of Muhammad, he was violently killed by Ali's opponents, the Sunnis of the Umayyad tribe.

Iblis: The Quranic name for Satan.

Ibn Ishaq: A Muslim scholar who recorded the story of the life of Prophet Muhammad (Siraht Rasul Allah).

Imam: A leader who has the authority to interpret the Islamic law. Shiites believe that the Imam is a political ruler, holds a manifestation of God, and through him alone the hidden knowledge and true meaning of the Quranic revelation can be known. They believe an Imam who disappeared in 874 A.D. and will some day come as the Mahdi.

Isa: The Arabic word for Jesus.

Islam: The religion revealed to Muhammad, the word means submission to the will of Allah and follow the teachings of the prophet Muhammad.

Islamic Movement of Uzbekistan; An Islamic terrorist group based in Tajikistan and its areas of operations include Uzbekistan, Tajikistan, Kyrgyz Stan and Afghanistan

Ishmael: The first son of Abraham by his wife's handmaid, Hagar. Muslims believe Ishmael, not Isaac, was the Son of God's promise to Abraham.

Israh: Ascension of Muhammad into the heavens companied by the Angel Gabriel during the Night Journey.

Israfil: The Angel of death companied by the Angle Gabriel

Jihad: Holy war, or sacred struggle in the sake of Allah.

Jinns: Spirit beings created by God, some are good and some are bad to humans.

Kaabah: A pre-Islamic cubical stone building, contains a black stone supposedly given by Adam by Gabriel and used by Abraham who allegedly built the Kaabah with his son Ishmael? The black stone was considered sacred and was kissed by Muhammad, and by Muslims since then.

Kafer: Unbeliever who do not believe in Allah and his Messenger Muhammad.

Khadijah: Muhammad's first wife, she was his only wife until her death in year 620 A.D.

Kufr: Infidelity or apostasy.

Kun-fa-Ykun: God's instant order for his creation, a verse in the Quran, He said, *"Be so it happened"*.

Library of Alexandria: An ancient historic library in the city of Alexandria, Egypt. The Library was burned when Omar Ibn Al Ass, the Arab Muslim leader reached Alexandria.

Mahdi: The guided one or coming world leader of righteousness. Sunnis wait for him to appear, and Shiites believe that the last Imam who disappeared 874 A.D. will some day appear as the Mahdi

Mamluks: An Islamic extreme armed group, which ruled Egypt, Syria and Palestine under the Ottoman Empire, originally slaves from Kosovo.

Mecca: The birthplace of Muhammad, the most holy city in Islam.

Medina: The second most holy city of Islam (after Mecca), previously an Oasis town named Yathrib where Muhammad fled to in 622 A.D.

Merriam: The Arabic name for Mary the Mother of Jesus.

Miraj: Muhammad's visit to Jerusalem coming back from heavens during the Night Journey.

Mongols: (AD, 1258-1369), under the leadership of Jinks Kahn, Invaded the Muslim territories and ended the reign of the Abbasids Caliphate, ruled from Sinai desert to India.

Mosque: A building where Muslims gather regularly for prayers.

Muhammad: The founder of Islam, born 570 AD and died 632 A.D. He is considered by the Muslims to be the last and final

Prophet of Allah through whom Allah gave the revelations in the Quran.

Muslim: A person who submits to Allah and follows the teachings of His Messenger Muhammad.

Nasikh-wa-Mansukh: A system of Quranic interpretation where newer verses cancel previous verses. (Abrogate and abrogated).

Napoleon Bonaparte: A French Army General and Emperor of France. Invaded Egypt in 1798, drove the Islamic extreme Mamluk's rule out of Egypt, he replaced the Islamic laws with civil laws taken after the French Constitution. The French occupation to Egypt for three short years marked the beginning of modern Egypt.

Nestor: A Patriarch of Constantinople, In 381 A.D., the Council of Ephesus was called to discuss his teachings that God the Word dwelt in the man Jesus, consequently, he denied that the person of Jesus to be called God and the Virgin Mary to be called the mother of God.

Nicene Creed: Was formed in 325 A.D. based on the teaching of an Alexandrian Deacon who would become Saint Athanasius the Apostolic, The creed is now recited throughout the Christian world which reads *"We believe in one God, God the Father the Almighty, creator of heaven and earth, and all things seen and unseen. We believe in one Lord Jesus Christ, the Only-Begotten Son of God, begotten of the Father before all ages; Light of Light, true God of true God, Begotten not created, of one Essence with the Father, by Whom all things were made; Who for us and for our salvation came down from Heaven, and was incarnate of the Holy Spirit and the Virgin Mary and became Man. He was crucified for us under Pontius Pilate, suffered and was buried. And in the third day He rose from the dead, according to the scriptures, ascended* *into the Heavens; He sits at the right hand of His Father, and He is coming again in His glory to judge the living and dead, Whose Kingdom shall have no end. Yes, we believe in the Holy Spirit, the Lord, the Life –Giver, Who proceeds from the father, Who with the Father and the Son is worshipped and glorified, Who spoke by the Prophets, And in One Holy, Catholic and Apostolic Church, We confess one Baptism for the remission of sins. We look for the resurrection of the dead, and the life of the coming age. Amen."*

Night Journey: A miraculous one night flight of Muhammad ascending into Heaven, Angel Gabriel took him in a ride over a human faced and winged horse to visit heaven and Hell and to meet Allah.

Ottman Empire: (1453-1924 A.D.), Conquered and captured Constantinople and put an end to the Byzantine Empire.

Pentagon: The Head Quarters of United States Department of Defense.

It was attacked by extremists on September 11,2001 (911).

People of the book: The Jews and Christian are so named by Muhammad in the Quran referring to the people of the Torah and The Gospel.

Qadar: Allah, His decree of good and evil, predetermines all things. ***Quibla***: Point of direction that Muslims turn to in prayer facing Mecca. ***Quran***: The Islamic sacred Holy book.

Quraysh: Powerful governing Pagan tribe of Mecca at the time of Muhammad, Muhammad's father Abdullah was a member of a clan of this tribe.

Ramadan: The ninth month of the Muslim calendar during which Muslims observe daily fasting from dawn to sun set.

Safa and Marwa: Two mountains near Mecca that during the Hajj Muslims go between them back and forth as Abram's second wife Hagar is believed to have done so during her search for water.

Salman Rushdie: Writer of the "Satanic Verses", a novel which caused the Ayatollah Khomeini of Iran to issue a Fatwa (legal verdict) sanctioning his death.

Satanic Verses: Quranic verses in which Muhammad recognized Idol Pagan Goddesses with intersession powers with Allah. Later said that Satan deceived him to pronounce that.

Shariah: Islamic law regarding the duties of Muslims toward Allah according to the Quran and Hadith (sayings of Muhammad).

Shihada: To bear witness reciting the creed "there is no god but Allah and Muhammad is the Messenger of Allah " saying it sincerely is all that necessary to become a Muslim.

Shi'ites or Shiites: A major Islamic sect, followers of Ali ibn Abu Talib, Cousin of Muhammad and his successor as the fourth Caliph. Shiites believe that the sure and true knowledge can come only through the guidance of the infallible Imam.

Sufism: A sect of Islam, Sufis reject the Quranic verses that refers to violence and they adapt mystical techniques and believe that a true spiritual state obtains knowledge directly from God.

Sunnis: Followers of Omar Ibn Al-Katab, successor of Muhammad as the Second caliph. Sunnis believe in the community as a source of guidance and knowledge driven from the Quran and Hadith sources.

Surah: A chapter of the Quran book, which include 114 Surahs.

Umayyah: A clan of the tribe of Quraysh.

Umayyed Caliphate: (661-750 A.D.), followed the rule of Uthman, the fourth Caliph.

Omar-Ibn Al-katab: He was the second Caliph, successor of Muhammad, Assassinated in 644 A.D.

Uthman ibn Affan: The third caliph, successor of Muhammad.

Taliban: An Islamic fundamentalist extreme movement that based in Afghanistan and was associated with the Saudi exile.

Wahhabi: 18th century puritanical movement founded by the Islamic reformer Muhammad-Ibn-Abd-Alwahhab (1703-1792) that became the official creed of the Saudi dynasty; adherents observe literalism and strict observance of pure version of Islam.

Waraka Ibn Nofel: Uncle of Khadijah, the first wife of Muhammad, he was a Nestorian Christian Bishop of Arabia, he blessed their marriage.

World Trade Center: Twin high-rise buildings in New York that were attacked by Muslim extremist on September 11, 2001 (911).

Yazidis: followers of Yazid, the son of Muawiya Ibn Abi Sufyan.

Yathrib: an ancient oasis in the Arabian Desert, to which Muhammad fled Escaping persecution from Mecca. Later named Medina (city of the Prophet).

Yehya: The Arabic name of John the Baptist in the Quran.

Yusef: The Arabic name of Joseph in the Quran.

Zakat: A religious offering of a devout Muslim given primarily to the poor and needy.

Zainab: Daughter of Muhammad from his first wife Khadijah.

Zechariah: Father of John the Baptist.

REFERENCES

PUBLISHED BOOK REFERENCES:

- Norman L. Geisler & Abdul Salib, Answering Islam, the Crescent in the light of the Cross, Baker Book House Co., 1993.

- Bernard Lewis, the Crises of Islam, Holy War and Unholy Terror, Random House Trade Paperbacks, New York, USA, 2005.

- Mark A. Gabriel, Ph.D., Islam and Terrorism, Charisma House, 2002.

- Mark A. Gabriel, Ph.D. Islam and the Jews, the Unfinished Battle, Charisma House, Lake Mary, Florida, USA, 2003.

- Reza F. Safa, Inside Islam, Exposing and Reaching the World of Islam, Charisma House, 1996.

- Encyclopedia Britannica, Islamic Myth and Legend (page 949) Helen Hemingway Benton, Publisher, Chicago/ London/ Toronto/ Geneva/ Sydney/Tokyo / Manila/ Seoul, 1973-1974.

- Andrew Rippin; Muslims, Their religions, Beliefs and Policies, Vol. I, Routledge, New York, NY, USA, 1990.

- Andrew Rippin; Muslims, Their religions, Beliefs and Policies, Vol. II, Routledge, New York, NY, USA, 1993.

- Mostafa Vaziri, The Emergence of Islam, Prophecy Imamate & Messianism in perspective, Paragon House, New York, N,Y.,1992.

- Muhammad Zafrulla Khan, The Quran, English and Arabic, Interlink Publishing Group, Inc., New York, NY, USA, 1970.

- Yahiya Emerick, the Life and Work of Mohammad, Alpha, a Pearson Education Company, Indianapolis, Indiana, USA, 2002.

- Mohammad Al Ghazoli, Christ, Mohammad & I, ISBN 0-7866-9 Copyright 2004.

- Aisha Abdul-Rahman (Bint Al Shati), Women of the Prophet, Cairo, Egypt, (Arabic)

INTERNET SITE REFERENCES:

- "http://www.answering-islam.org/"p://www.answering-islam.org

- "http://www.zombietime.com/Mohammed_image_Archive/"p://www.Zombietime.com/Mohammed_image_Archive/

- "http://en.wikipedia.org/"p://en.wikipedia.org

- "http://canadiancoalition.com/"p://canadiancoalition.com

- "http://www.memritv.org/"p://www.memritv.org

- "http://www.islamundressed.com/"p://www.Islamundressed.com

- "http://www.newadvent.org/"p://www.newadvent.org

- "http://www.obsessionthemovie.com/"p://www.obsession-themovie.com

- "http://itl.org.uk/"p://itl.org.uk

- "http://www.usc.edu/dept/msa/"p://www.usc.edu/dept/msa/

- "http://www.explorefaith.org/"p://www.explorefaith.org

- "http://www.grace-and-truth.org/"p://www.Grace-and-truth.org

www.ingramcontent.com/pod-product-compliance
Lightning Source LLC
Chambersburg PA
CBHW021615120626
46545CB00001B/243